UNFINISHED WORK

Letters in Defense of Israel, the Jewish People and the Truth

LEN BENNETT

D1572623

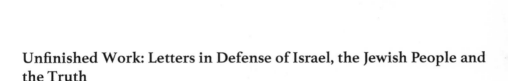

Unfinished Work: Letters in Defense of Israel, the Jewish People and the Truth
©2019 Len Bennett

ISBN Paperback: 978-1-9991056-0-0
ISBN eBook: 978-1-9991056-2-4

POLITICAL SCIENCE / International Relations / General
POLITICAL SCIENCE / Political Ideologies / General
POLITICAL SCIENCE / Civil Rights

LETTERS BY YEAR

This book is dedicated to my darling wife, Paula,
my daughter, Randi,
and my nieces and nephews,
Robyn, Neil, Lorry, Deborah, Emily,
Carly, Brianna, Megan, Miles,
Jacki, Harper and Meritt.

PREFACE

I was born in Montreal just before the start of World War II. I remember rationing and coupon booklets, blackouts and air raid sirens. Jews were being slaughtered in Europe. My government seemed not to know.

I remember the declaration of the State of Israel. My father said it was a bad idea. I disagreed.

Soon after, two young cousins, Rhoda and Laura, emigrated to Israel and lived on kibbutzim.

I visited in 1969.

I stayed with a friend, Marsha, in Ramat Aviv. I walked the empty roads to Tel Aviv beach on Yom Kippur, getting directions en route from a cotton farmer. We conversed in French.

I loved everything.

I've had a subscription to the Jerusalem Post ever since.

Back home, Yahoo sent me unsolicited newspaper articles on the Middle East from around the world, some of which struck me as biased. I decided to write and set the record straight.

I attempted to be apolitical and focus on issues.

I am deeply grateful to the editors who found my letters sufficiently interesting, enlightening or provocative to accept them.

"A conflict begins and ends in the hearts and minds of people, not in the hilltops." —Amos Oz

1988

Man's Inhumanity
Ottawa Citizen, March 2, 1988

It is long overdue that the school system in the nation's capital will finally inform its children of the most heinous event the world has witnessed.

The Holocaust represents the only time that a nation, for no political gain, set out to exterminate a minority within its own population.

The tragedy of the Jews of Europe was compounded by a world that looked away when the storm was gathering. The anti-Semitism in Canada, which kept of Jews from safety in this country, contributed to the tragedy.

The Holocaust should be treated as a unique phenomenon.

While the study of man's inhumanity to man is important, the Holocaust, as the culmination of 1,500 years of anti-Semitism must receive special attention.

Other events pale in comparison.

"When people criticize Zionists, they mean Jews. You're talking anti-Semitism." —Martin Luther King

---

1989

Israel's Record
Ottawa Citizen, January 1989

In I.M.'s letter, a trade question becomes the excuse for the claim that "Israel has been condemned by the international community for its subjugation of the Palestinians and human rights violations".

I would like to update Mr. M. On some of the "violations" that have occurred since Israel occupied the territories 20 years ago.

In 1968, the gross domestic product of the West Bank and Gaza was $441 million. By 1986, this quadrupled to $1.5 billion. Unemployment, 18 percent in Gaza and 13.5 percent in the West Bank, decreased to 1.5 and three percent respectively.

The percentage of working-age men with greater than elementary school education rose between 1970 and 1984 from 22 to 44 percent in the West Bank and from 32 to 52 percent in Gaza. There were no universities or vocational schools in 1967. There are now six universities and 24 vocational schools.

In 1985, 93 percent of households in Gaza had electricity compared to 23 percent in 1972; 77 percent had TV sets (eight percent in 1972); and 78 percent had refrigerators (six percent in 1972). The West Bank went from owning 1,600 private cars in 1970 to 35,000 in 1986.

In 21 years, the West Bank increased its exports 20-fold, selling $239 million worth of goods in 1986, mostly to Israel and Jordan, and 115,000 Gazans and West Bankers were employed in Israel, earning nearly double the rate in the territories.

The infant mortality rate dropped from 87 per 1,000 to 26 per 1,000 in the past 21 years, probably the best rate in the Arab world.

These impressive achievements stand in contrast to the neighboring Arab countries, are the result of the huge benefits conferred on both Israel and the territories by their economic co-operation and peaceful coexistence.

PLO's Terrorism
Ottawa Citizen, March 27, 1989

There is no reason why Canada should rush into recognition of the PLO.

Joe Clark's statement that the PLO has been making strides towards peace skews the reality in the Middle East.

Arafat, after years of double-talk, uttered the magic words that allowed the U.S. to enter into tenuous discussions with him. He rejected terrorism "in all its forms".

He has not been true to his word.

Bethlehem Mayor Elias Freij proposed a one-year UN-sponsored truce in the territories to allow negotiations to begin in a calmer atmosphere. Arafat responded that any Palestinian leader who proposed an end to the intifada exposed himself to the bullets of his own people". Palestinian activist Faisel Husseini, on his release from jail, recommended that local elections be held on the West Bank and Gaza. He was quickly forced to say that elections could only be held after the withdrawal of Israeli troops.

Three times in southern Lebanon, Israeli troops apprehended PLO terrorists on their way to attack civilian targets in Israel.

Finally, evidence in the air disaster over Scotland points to a group under the PLO.

Arafat represents the PLO or he doesn't. He has to be for peace or not. The purpose of the intifada is to kill Jews. The purpose of blowing up aircraft is to show that democracies are vulnerable.

Canada should play a positive role in solving the Arab-Israeli conflict. It should demand that all terrorism be terminated as the price for Canadian recognition of the PLO.

MID-EAST CONFLICT
Ottawa Citizen, November, 1989

Abdullah Abdullah's letter holds a whisper of truth among the many falsehoods. The Palestinians have indeed had many "experts" speaking for them: the King of Jordan, who rules a country that is 60-percent Palestinian; the president of Syria, who is destroying the Lebanese Christian community and who considers Lebanon and Israel to be part of Syria; the PLO and others.

Now a new group has been heard from – the residents of the West Bank and Gaza, who started the intifada because they had no faith in the PLO, and were ignored by the Arab League.

The residents of the territories deserve to have their voices heard in finding an accommodation with Israel that will allow them to exercise their own aspirations, while reassuring Israel that another Lebanon will not be created.

The Arab-Israeli conflict can be solved when the 22-member Arab League meets Israel to end 40 years of hostilities. The UN can only play a limited role in ending this conflict, until it removes from its record its biased, anti-Semitic, resolutions. Hopefully, Canada, while on the Security Council, can be influential in this regard.

Mark Twain on Palestine: "...(a) desolate country whose soil is rich enough, but is given over wholly to weeds-a silent mournful expanse....We never saw a human being on the whole route...There was hardly a tree or a shrub anywhere. Even the olive and the cactus, those fast friends of worthless soil, had almost deserted the country."

1991

MIDDLE EAST ISSUES
Ottawa Citizen, April 26, 1991

Will the Palestinians lose again? Will they once again be frustrated? Will the current window of opportunity slam shut? Will Canada urge her Arab coalition partners to recognize history, accept peace, and not repeat the errors of the past? In the wake of the Gulf War an opportunity exists to solve the Arab-Israeli conflict. The biggest winners of an agreement would be the Palestinians.

There are a number of facts that the Arabs, including the Palestinians, must accept. To begin with, Israel has something that the Arabs want – land. The Arabs have nothing to offer Israel, other than an end to hostilities and terrorism. Israel is not going to deal with the Tunis-based PLO, so another Palestinian leadership will have to be developed.

Israel is not going to accept a United Nations role. There are 50 members of the UN that have either Muslim majorities or significant Muslim minorities.

The way to peace is as follows: Israel and its Arab neighbors must meet and offer each other recognition and an end to hostilities. They must encourage, and assist in developing, an indigenous Palestinian leadership. The intifada must stop, so that normal interaction can resume between Israel and the territories.

The result will be redrawn, secure, recognized borders between Israel and a Palestinian, or Jordanian-Palestinian entity in the West Bank and Gaza.

The Palestinian area will be autonomous and demilitarized. Israeli settlements in the region will give Israel the confidence that the agreement will be honored. In order to guarantee that all religions will continue to enjoy free access to their holy places in Jerusalem, Jerusalem will remain united and the capital of Israel.

After a few years, the Palestinians can decide for themselves what type of country they want.

1992

RACISM AND THE CITIZEN
Ottawa Citizen, January 20, 1992

The Jan. 7 editorial on racism in Israel says more about the *Citizen's* editorial policy than it does about Israel. If, as you maintain, some of Israel's acts are "irredeemably racist," what must you think of some of Canada's acts?

Were Israel to capture Arab children and send them for adoption in the U.S., as Canada did with Indian children in the 1970s, that would be racism. Where Israel to take Arab children away from their families and villages, send them to residential schools, and force them to learn the "right" language and religion, beating them when they spoke their own tongue or spoke to their siblings, such as Canada did with our native children until the 1970s, that would be racism. Law-abiding Arabs in Israel do not fear the police, as do blacks in Montreal and Toronto.

If you see differences between the treatment of Israelis and Arabs, it may be that you are selective, and possibly loose with the facts. For example, the 12 Palestinians who are to be deported are not the innocents you make them out to be. Two have previously been sentenced for murder and were released during a prisoner exchange.

The intifada has made life difficult for the Arabs in the territories. Under previous regimes, under the control of Turkey, Britain, Jordan and Egypt, they were very harshly treated. Since 1967, with cooperation between Israel and Jordan, their standard of living has soared, with hospitals, universities and trade schools being established. They were not independent, but they were certainly better off than their neighbors.

I can conceive of no country treating an insurrection with as much self-control and as little force as Israel has.

Last year at Oka, we again used massive force, even preventing food and medicine from getting into the village. Fortunately, the UN was looking the other way.

At best, I consider your editorial to be "chutzpah". Others may consider it to be racist.

JUST PROPAGANDA
Ottawa Citizen, June 8, 1992

The May 26 article by Robert Fisk, "The Killing of Innocents," should have been labeled *propaganda* rather than *opinion*. I have difficulty understanding why the *Citizen* would allow such biased drivel to masquerade as news.

The article describes in elaborate detail the families of Hezbollah terrorists who are caught up in the violence created by their fathers. The author places in quotations any comments from Israeli sources, so the reader understands that the explanations are of dubious veracity. Where were Mr. Fisk's gory descriptions of the 15-year-old Israeli schoolgirl or the rabbi who were stabbed to death by Arabs the same week?

Has he written a condemnation of the recent bombing of an Israeli embassy?

Fisk's article shows how selective juxtaposition of facts, quotes out of context, and opinions solicited from fringe personalities can give a distorted picture. I expect more of the *Citizen*.

1993

HATS OFF TO THE RUSSIANS
Ottawa Citizen, November 17, 1993

There is little that we can learn from the Russians, but they do have something most Canadians would envy, particularly as we enter the election campaign.

It is a program called No Comment, in which viewers can watch a news event without any editorial interference. There are no reporters' questions or comments. On the screen appear the date and location of the news item. For example, if the event is a speech or discussion, the viewer hears only the speakers and comments from the crowd or participants.

Wouldn't it be wonderful if we could follow the federal campaign and make up our own minds without having the media and the pollsters masticate and regurgitate everything for us?

"Some people like the Jews, and some do not. But no thoughtful man can deny that they are, beyond any question, the most formidable and most remarkable race which has appeared in the world."—Winston Churchill

---

2003

THE TRUTH AT CONCORDIA

Jerusalem Post, March 7, 2003

On Monday, September 9, I had a ticket to hear Benjamin Netanyahu speak at Concordia University.

Knowing there would be protests, I went early and spent about 3/4 of an hour talking to some of the protesters. They were waving Palestinian and Che Guevera flags and chanting and screaming. Most just kept repeating mantras and didn't know what they were talking about. Others were very anti-Semitic.

Some were just having a good time and others felt that if Israel was nice, everything would be OK.

There was university and police security. The protesters were on one street, and the line for ticket holders was on another.

I was already in the auditorium when a group of Arabs stormed the people in line, hitting, spitting, and generally scaring those waiting. Eventually, the police separated those trying to get in from those trying to violently prevent them from hearing Netanyahu.

Very slowly, the hall started to fill up. Then we heard that there was a riot outside. The so-called student protesters broke a few big windows, stormed into closed areas of the buildings, broke up furniture and threw chairs and other items at the police.

Pepper spray and/or tear gas was used.

The (incompetent) security forces finally decided that they could not control the mob, and the speech was canceled. Some 650 people in the auditorium were kept hostage for about four hours, until we were able to leave, under police escort, in small groups. Many kids were frightened.

It was a sad day for the university, the police and free speech. It was a good day for Arab thugs.

GROUPS ARE FINGERS ON THE SAME HAND
Sun Sentinel, April 9, 2003

Two articles, one in the Monday Forum ("Civil liberties," by T.D. and an editorial, (Criticize allies, don't boycott") miss a very important issue.

The security services of the U.S., Canada, France, Germany, Russia, Italy and others have been working together for years. They share intelligence on terrorist regimes and organizations and work together to combat them. They have known for years that all the terrorists worldwide cooperate with each other when it is in their interests. They all, including France, know that Carlos (the Jackal), the Baader-Meinhof gang, Iraq, Syria, Iran, Hezbollah and others are fingers on the same hand – or perhaps that should be fist.

So, the United States is not putting aside the "war on terrorism" to fight Iraq. The war in Iraq is an integral part of the war on terrorism. As for France, it deserves a good kick in the wine and cheese.

As a Canadian, I am ashamed of my country for sitting on the fence and for booing the American anthem at hockey games. My mother was an American, and as such I am proud of President Bush and the American people. They and their allies are keeping the world safe for democracy.

NO RIGHT OF RETURN
Canadian Jewish News, August 7, 2003

Andy Lehrer's letter is rather simplistic. There is no "right of return" for anyone under international law.

I have no "right of return" to Russia or to the United States, where my family emigrated from. My wife has no "right of return" to Ukraine. The 900,000 Jews who were forced out of the Arab lands after 1947 have no "right of return." The 700,000 Lebanese Christians who fled the Palestinian occupation of southern Lebanon in the 1970s have few rights. (The Palestinians were thrown out of Jordan after a failed uprising against the Hashemite king).

On the other hand, Israel's Law of Return recognizes the hardships and anti-Semitism many Jews have faced and offers them a home. Thus, Jews forced out of Arab lands as well as Ethiopia, the former Soviet Union and, more recently, France and Argentina, are now safe in Israel.

As for the population of the region 100 years ago, it was very sparse. There were Arabs and Jews who had lived there forever, but 70% of the people who today call themselves Palestinians came to the area for economic reasons from other Arab lands, following the migration of eastern European Jews that began in 1880.

Today, 50 per cent of Israeli Jews originally came from Arab lands. The Palestinian refugees are kept in camps because Arab leaders refuse to take them into their own countries. Israel has no obligation to compensate the refugees, but it should get together with the Arab countries and establish a fund to compensate both Arab and Jewish refugees, and the Arab countries should accept their brothers into their countries.

"There is no difference whatever between anti-Semitism and the denial of Israel's statehood. Classical anti-Semitism denies the equal right of Jews as citizens within society. Anti-Zionism denies the equal rights of the Jewish people its lawful sovereignty within the community of nations. The common principle in the two cases is discrimination." —Abba Eban

---

2004

READ BY BILL O'REILLY
The O'Reilly Factor, February 25, 2004

Len, Deerfield Beach, Florida. I'm withholding his last name.

Mr. Gibson is a racist. No one but the victims of Christian dogma have the right to define anti-Semitism. Not you O'Reilly and not Gibson.

REFUGEES FLED JORDAN, NOT ISRAEL
Montreal Gazette, September, 2004

A. M.'s article, "Palestinian infighting erupts at refugee camp", both informs and misinforms.

He notes that there are Palestinian refugee camps in Lebanon controlled by Lebanese army checkpoints, that rival groups and terrorists clash for power, that targeted assignations are common, that fugitives from justice are protected and that innocent civilians might get caught in the crossfire.

However, these are not refugees from Israel's war of independence. These are the refugees from Black September, the civil war that Yasser Arafat's Palestinian Liberation Organization waged unsuccessfully against the Hashemite Kingdom of Jordan in the 1970s.

In Lebanon, they occupied much of the south of the country, imposed taxes and terrorized the local Christian population. They fought on the Muslim side during the Lebanese civil war, helping to drive 700,000 Christians out of the country.

It was the Syrian occupation of Lebanon that curtailed the Palestinian's power, and they were confined to refugee camps.

"If we bear all this suffering and if there
are still Jews left, when it is over, then Jews,
instead of being doomed, will be held up as an
example." —Anne Frank

2005

Israeli Unilateralism Is Testing The Limits Of Human Patience
Daily Star, Lebanon, July 20, 2005

It is the Palestinian unilateralism that created the instability of the past four years. It was Yasser Arafat's rejection of Camp David and the Taba talks and his starting of the latest intifada, which led to the present situation.

The PA was responsible for 95 percent of Palestinians before Camp David. Arafat's intifada led to Israel's separation barrier. With Arafat's death, hope was renewed, but Mahmoud Abbas has yet to take the first step in the "road map" – the dismantling and disarming of Hamas, Islamic Jihad, etc.

Israel's unilateral actions are in response to the PA's unwillingness to negotiate and put an end to violence. The Arab and Islamic world can play a key role in advising its Palestinian friends in the region against taking self-destructive, unilateral measures that will undermine the road to peace. It is in everyone's interest in the region to have sincere and bilateral dialogue. By encouraging the PA to halt terrorism, the Arabs can help the Israelis secure hitherto absent Palestinian partners for peace.

Tolerating Racism Leads To Violence Against Its Victims
Montreal Gazette, July 17, 2005

Charles Moore, you have "The freedom to be wrong," and you are wrong.

The more racism and hatred are tolerated, even under the guise of freedom of speech, the more violence will be perpetuated against its victims.

While rational, educated people may write off Ahenakew as a bigot, others will take his ranting as support for violence.

Most hate crimes in Canada are directed against Jewish targets. If you need the freedom to express hatred, pick on someone your own size. There are a billion Catholics, a billion Hindus and 1.4 billion Muslims. Racism may hurt them, but not as much as it does the small Jewish community. During my lifetime, one out of every three Jews in the world were murdered. Their numbers have yet to recover.

Kids in Canada have to know: We are a tolerant society, but we will not tolerate racism.

IRANIAN LEADER IGNORES HISTORY
Sun-Sentinel, December 15, 2005

Iran's President Mahmoud Ahmadinejad believes that, because of the Holocaust, Israel should be removed to Europe.

He ignores the fact that during World War II, Lebanon, Syria, Iraq, Egypt and the Arabs of Palestine were all Nazi supporters. In Fact, the grand mufti of Jerusalem spent the war years in Berlin as the personal guest of Hitler, planning the "final solution" for the Jews of the Middle East. He was also personally responsible for the deaths of 3000 Jewish Hungarian children when he learned of a plan to ransom them. He appealed to Hitler, and the plan was thwarted, the children being sent to death camps.

The Jews of Palestine were the only Middle Easterners to support the Allies and to send troops to fight the Nazis.

After the Arab nations rejected the U.N. Partition Plan and initiated repeated genocidal wars of aggression against Israel, Israel has earned the right to live in peace in the Middle East.

As for the plight of the Palestinians languishing in Arab countries, Khaled Al-Azm, Syria's prime minister after the 1948 war, stated in his 1972 memoirs:

"Since 1948, it is we who demanded the return of the refugees... while it is we who made them leave...We brought disaster upon Arab refugees, by inviting them and bringing pressure to bear upon them to leave...We have rendered them dispossessed...We have accustomed them to begging...We have participated in lowering their moral and social level...Then we exploited them in executing crimes of murder, arson and throwing bombs upon...men, women and children—all of this in the service of political purposes."

"It is not the strongest of the species that survive, nor the most intelligent, but the one most responsive to change." —Charles Darwin

---

2006

WILL OLMERT MAKE HISTORY, OR WILL HE SOW THE SEEDS OF FUTURE CONFLICT?
Daily Star, Lebanon, March 28, 2006

Perhaps it is time for the King of Saudi Arabia to play the role of Egyptian President Anwar Sadat. Let the King phone the Israeli Prime Minister, come to Jerusalem and address the Knesset. Let him propose his plan, listen to the Israeli counter-proposal, and negotiate a resolution that will give neither the Arabs nor the Israelis everything they want, but enough to satisfy them both.

The huge, oil-rich Arab world should be generous to tiny Israel. Arabs have the support of the Islamic world, and the rest of the world's Middle Eastern policies are based on keeping oil flowing.

Israel and the Palestinians have much in common. 50% of today's Israelis and Palestinians are the descendants of immigrants from the Arab world in the last century.

The Islamic world must remove anti-Semitism from school books, mosques and government-controlled media. They must forgo suicide-bombers and terrorism as means of negotiating. They must accept that Jews have a right to be part of the Middle East.

After that, a peaceful resolution to all issues will be easy.

"There is no security on the Earth, there is only opportunity." —Douglas MacArthur

---

2007

A Fair Palestinian-Israeli Peace Deal Might Partly Salvage Bush's Legacy
Daily Star, Lebanon, February 8, 2007

George Bush will just bump into a wall, as did Bill Clinton. So long as Iran and Syria sponsor terrorism and the Palestinians fight each other, there is no possible end to the Arab-Israeli conflict.

Where are the Arab leaders who can prevail upon the Palestinian leaders to stop shooting and to start talking, both to themselves and to the Israelis? Is there anyone in the Arab world who really cares about the Palestinians? Is there anyone who wants to see a free and independent Palestine next to Israel? Is there anyone in the Arab world who will stop using the Palestinians as a tool and who has the influence to move towards peace?

Where are the Arab leaders who care about their own legacies?

Will Arab Leaders Spare A Thought For The Consequences Of Their Misrule?
Daily Star, Lebanon, July 2, 2007

It is refreshing to read an editorial that places the blame for the ills of the Arab world on their leaders, and does not demonize the West or Israel for the hardships that most Arabs live under. It is time for men of good will to stop the incitement against Israel and Western societies and to focus on creating Islamic countries that Muslims will want to emigrate to.

"The greatest danger for most of us is not that our aim is too high and we miss it, but that it is too low and we reach it." —Michelangelo

---

2008

EXULT IN FREEDOM
Sun-Sentinel, January 04, 2008

As a non-Christian and non-American, I am annoyed by the complaint in the Dec. 27 letter, "Holiday hoo-hah" that Christmas is a national holiday, while the letter writer's own holiday is not.

I am grateful to be here. If America rejects its Christian heritage, radical Islam will take over, as it is doing in Europe and elsewhere. The Dutch are fleeing Amsterdam. Ten Jews are attacked in the streets of Paris every day. Eighty percent of Bethlehem's Christians have been forced out since the Palestinian Authority took over in the 1990s. Nearly a million Jews have fled the Arab world since the 1940s. Christians fled the Palestinian occupation of Lebanon in the 1970s. This year, in the 10 days that Ramadan overlapped with the Jewish High Holy Days, there were 94 Islamist terror attacks worldwide.

Sure, the incessant Christmas carols after Thanksgiving can grate on the nerves, but the freedom America offers demands that we accommodate each other and appreciate our diversity.

The letter writer is like the guest at a wedding so perfect that the only complaint is that the bride is too beautiful.

NEXT CHALLENGE FOR THE GOVERNMENT
Dominion Post, New Zealand, March 3, 2008

Now that Wellington has hosted a conference on the use of cluster bombs, it is time to deal with a more serious menace.

The major cause of death and injury to innocent civilians is the use of suicide bombers by terrorists.

The civilized world must condemn them and the organizations and governments that support and foster them.

The cluster-bomb issue is the low-hanging fruit. Now let's see if New Zealand has the gumption and capacity to go after the main source of death and injury to innocent men, women and children.

WITHOUT UNITY, PALESTINIANS HAVE NO WAY TO FEND OFF ISRAELI WAR CRIMES"
Daily Star, Lebanon, June 12, 2008

The real problem in Gaza is the Hamas terrorist entity. Gaza is under control of a regime that cares nothing for its people. Their only focus is on the death and destruction of innocent civilians. They care little for the suffering of Gazans. Rather than enjoy the freedom offered when Israel withdrew from Gaza, they destroyed the greenhouses and buildings left for them, and attacked any Arab opposition to their dictatorial rule.

This is the same mentality that occupied much of Lebanon in the 1970s, when the PLO taxed the Lebanese, harassed the population and contributed greatly to the Civil War that forced out 700,000 Lebanese Christians. The media tends to forget that this is the reason the Palestinians, who occupy 12 enclaves in Lebanon where the government is forbidden from entering, are now denied basic civil rights by the Lebanese.

Where is the fabled Arab hospitality? Where is the generosity toward their own brothers? Where is the welcome to the stranger? Surely 1.2 billion Muslims can accept a tiny Jewish state and a Palestinian state living side by side.

MORAL DEGENERATION OF TERRORISTS
Canadian Jewish News, August 7, 2008

Body counts and the number of prisoners held is not a measure of any conflict ("Israel, Hezbollah reach prisoner swap,) That is like saying that Canada is bad because we have more murderers in our prisons than policemen. Israel is a country, and one of the oldest in the United Nations. It has legitimate rights and obligations under international law. It is obligated to defend its citizens from non-governmental groups such as Hamas, Hezbollah and Islamic Jihad, all recognized as terrorist organizations by the civilized world. That Lebanon, under Iranian/Syrian control, occupied by Hezbollah and the 12 Palestinian enclaves, celebrated the return of a child killer speaks to their moral degeneration.

Arabs Need To Act, Too
Montreal Gazette, September 17, 2008

Your article focuses on what a new Israeli leader could do to inject a little hope into the Middle East, but is silent on what actions might be taken from the Arab side.

The 22 members of the Arab League could immediately take a number of steps if they are interested in an independent Palestinian state living in peace adjacent to the state of Israel.

They could denounce terrorism against Israelis and Jews. They could announce their readiness to resolve issues peacefully. They could stop the virulent anti-Semitism that is pervasive in their media, schools and mosques. They could stop their international campaign of harassment against Jews and Israel on campuses, in trade unions and at the United Nations. They could recognize the ethnic cleansing of 900,000 Jews from the Arab world and Iran since the 1940s and absorb into their countries Arab refugees in a quid pro quo.

The Arab League has treated the Palestinians shamefully. They have denied them citizenship, except for Jordan, and forced them to live in a state of uncertainty for all these years.

The question is whether the Arab League wants the Palestinians to have a home or do they just want to keep the pot boiling to mask their own inadequacies and conflicts.

"Be the change that you wish to see in the world." —Mahatma Gandhi

---

2009

PART OF THE PROPAGANDA?
Gulf Daily News, Bahrain, March 10, 2009

With reference to the column 'Zionist taboo persecuting critics,' academia in America is overwhelmingly left wing.

It is almost impossible for a conservative professor to get a posting.

If American universities were controlled by the right wingers, why are "Israel Apartheid Weeks" tolerated when it is obvious that Israel is the only non-apartheid country in the Middle East.

It is because the anti-Vietnam era pot smokers are now the professors in control that such racism can flourish under the guise of freedom of speech.

That a few conservative voices can be heard, and a few terror-supporters are pointed out, is the exception to the rule.

You seem to be too far away from the democratic world to have any sense of what is going on here.

Or, perhaps, you are just part of the Islamic propaganda machine.

"We can easily forgive a child who is afraid of the dark; the real tragedy of life is when men are afraid of the light." —Plato

2010

The First Holocaust
National Post, January 4, 2010

I find the "my tragedy was worse than your tragedy" arguments to be most unsavory. The 20th century saw Europe masticate itself. The Holocaust differed from other genocides in that Europe murdered most of its Jews. Europe slaughtered one out of every three Jews in the entire world. This is a magnitude unheard of, and one from which the Jewish population has yet to recover.

Carter's Apology Falls Flat
Sun-Sentinel, January 31, 2010

I strongly disagree with Abraham Foxman's assessment of Jimmy Carter's so-called apology. Carter offers an Al Het prayer as a sop to the Jewish community. But what was he apologizing for? He was not begging forgiveness for the blatant lie he used to hustle his book, comparing Israel's treatment of West Bank Arabs with apartheid. He was not begging forgiveness because his promotion of this libel has caught on with organizations that spread anti-Semitism on university campuses across America. He apologized that he upset Jews. He apologized because he believes Jews are too sensitive. This is like apologizing for upsetting your wife when you beat her, rather than admitting your own brutality. If Carter ever feels guilty for his anti-Semitic ranting, he can apologize.

48 Responses To "A Botched Raid, A Vital Embargo"
New York Times, June 3, 2010

Israel was suckered.

Israeli intelligence should have known that this was a set-up. They know that Turkey has been cozying up with Iran, and Turkey and IHH were complicit in this venture.

They should have been prepared to meet the terrorists.

As for the world condemnation, what's new?

The Useless Nations are dominated by the 56-member Muslim block.

Europe's 50 million Muslims force the governments to condemn Israel or face riots.

So Israel can either defend herself or commit suicide. The US, Canada, the Netherlands and Italy understand this.

Misplaced Zeal
Montreal Gazette, July 15, 2010

Re: Ottawa should respect the Charter and bring Khadr home.

Irwin Cutler's zeal in demanding Omar Khadr's repatriation from Guantanamo Bay is excessive. Kahdr's trial might be the first of a child soldier in modern history, but he cannot realistically be seen as a child victim to be rehabilitated. As a member of "the first family of terrorism" what conceivable rehabilitation could he receive?

The "child soldier" designation was meant for children who were abducted and forced into military service and who had no control over their circumstances. This is not Khadr's situation.

The Supreme Court, wisely, did not order repatriation and deferred to the government to fashion a remedy. And surely taxpayer expense should not be a factor in any decision.

Any mistreatment Khadr might have suffered, does not mean that he should be freed. He should receive a trial as soon as possible that will determine his fate.

Cause Of Our Embroilment Is Arab Oil, Not Israel
Boston Globe, August 29, 2010

I take strong exception to Brian Nolen's statement, "Our government's blind allegiance to the so-called 51st state of Israel has caused immeasurable financial and emotional hardship for our country, and embroiled us in the perpetual turmoil that is the modern Middle East."

The foreign policies of all Western nations have always been based on the need to keep Arab oil flowing to the West. The major focus of US foreign policy is the coddling of Saudi Arabia, not Israel. George Bush held hands with, and Barack Obama bowed down to, the Saudi king.

Osama bin Laden never mentioned the Arab-Israeli conflict as a reason for 9/11. He was angered by US involvement and influence in the Arab world, particularly in Saudi Arabia. Bin Laden only jumped on the Palestinian issue after seeing them celebrating 9/11, and realizing that the fractious, feudal Muslims could only agree on one thing, that being the hatred of the "little Satan."

Have you ever considered that part of the reason Israel is hated is that it is the only reliable Middle East ally of the "great Satan"? Perhaps that's why the Islamic world is so hostile.

Hamas Gets PR Coup In Blockade
Sun-Sentinel, October 17, 2010

It is absolutely untrue that criticism of Israel generates "frequently unfounded and unnecessarily pushed 'anti-Jewish' panic button(s)." The reality is that anti-Semites generally are allowed to spew bias without being challenged. The Turkish ship was not unarmed, and the writer knows that by now. The IHH terrorist group planned this win-win situation for themselves. Either the blockade would be broken and Iran could arm its Hamas flunkies, or the Israelis would respond to being attacked on the ship and people would be hurt, giving the terrorists a PR victory. They bragged of becoming Shaheeds. Gaza is under collective punishment by Hamas who violently took over and controls the population. Even the UN is threatened, as in the recent cases of two UN summer camps that were torched by Hamas and the UN staff was threatened with death if they rebuild. Hamas doesn't want Gaza's children to have a little fun and respite from the summer heat. This is an outrage. This is collective punishment.

OBAMA'S MIDEAST PEACE GAME
U.S. News & World Report, November 11, 2010

Israeli Prime Minister Binyamin Netanyahu does not realize that the Middle East game has changed ["Negotiating Peace Should Be a Private Process."] No American administration and no Arab negotiator has ever made settlements out to be the critical issue. Mutual recognition, the end of hostilities, the borders separating Israel and Palestine, and refugees were the problems to be solved. Barack Obama changed all that. He, like former President Jimmy Carter, sees the Middle East conflict from a distinctly Arab perspective. Obama lavishes praise on the Arabs and misses no opportunity to scold Israel. His philosophy seems to be that if only Israel were more cooperative and did whatever the Arabs wanted, the Arabs would reciprocate. So he has scant praise for Israel unilaterally setting a 10-month construction freeze, while the Palestinians name public places after terrorists. Now Palestinian President Mahmoud Abbas threatens to quit peace talks unless the construction freeze is made permanent. The focus of the talks should be to set borders, allowing each side to build on its own territory. One must conclude that, even with a sympathetic American administration backing them, the Arabs are still not interested in allowing a Jewish state to exist.

READERS' TAKE ON GEORGE GALLOWAY
Ottawa Citizen, November 26, 2010

George Galloway's support for terrorism is well founded. He supports Hamas as the democratically elected government of 1.6 million Palestinians in Gaza. They won the most seats in the Palestinian elections, which included the West Bank and Gaza, but seized control of Gaza violently, murdering Fatah supporters and driving their opponents out of the territory. Thousands of Bedouin fled to Israel for safety.

His assertion that the so-called Israeli-Palestinian dispute is "the center of the confrontation between the Muslim and non-Muslim world" is disingenuous.

Solving the Arab-Israeli issues will have no effect on the myriad hatreds and rivalries in the feudal Middle East. It won't impact radical Islam's goal of undermining the West and establishing an Islamic caliphate.

He refers to Gaza as a "concentration-camp," inviting a Nazi comparison, a clearly anti-Semitic statement.

Galloway should be reminded of what Khaled Al-Azm, Syria's prime minister after the 1948 war, stated in his 1972 memoirs:

"Since 1948, it is we who demanded the return of the refugees .... while it is we who made them leave .... We brought disaster upon Arab refugees, by inviting them and bringing pressure to bear upon them to leave .... We have rendered them dispossessed .... We have accustomed them to begging .... We have participated in lowering their moral and social level .... Then we exploited them in executing crimes of murder, arson and throwing bombs upon .... men, women and children -- all of this in the service of political purposes."

To allow five million Palestinians into Israel will not satisfy the Sunni/Shiite conflict or Arab/Persian rivalries. Nor will it solve the issues of the 850,000 Jews driven from their homes in Arab countries or the 700,000 Christians forced out by the Palestinian occupation of Lebanon in the 1970s.

Galloway advocates for one democratic state from the Jordan River to the Mediterranean, with equal rights for Jews, Muslims and Christians.

The Muslims will not tolerate it. The Jews will flee for their lives and the Israeli Christian community, the only one currently growing in the Middle East, will follow suit.

As for the Bedouin, the Bahia, the gays, the Somali refugees and others who found safe haven in Israel, they will be once again in danger.

THOUGHTS ON THE MIDDLE EAST PEACE PROCESS
Guardian, UK, December 28, 2010

Tony Blair is an astute analyst of the Arab/Palestinian/Israeli conflict. However, I disagree with the assessment "that the American decision a fortnight ago to abandon attempts to pressure Israel to agree to a new partial freeze on construction in Jewish settlements was a 'setback' for attempts to get negotiations started again."

No previous American administration and no Arab negotiator has ever made settlements out to be *the* critical issue. Mutual recognition, the end of hostilities, the borders separating Israel and Palestine and refugees were the problems to be solved.

The Israelis had unilaterally implemented a 10-month freeze to induce the Palestinians to join peace talks. Now Obama asked the Israelis for an additional three-month construction freeze, and offered aid to both the Israelis and the Palestinians. The Israelis did not reject the package. They requested the offer in a letter, which the Americans did not produce. The question unanswered is whether the Palestinians agreed to return to the peace table in return for a freeze, or was this just Obama's wishful thinking.

Abbas has repeatedly stated that a construction freeze was required before he would continue peace talks. If Abbas did not agree to the three-month plan, then the offer was a major Obama diplomatic blunder, as was his making of settlements a key issue in the first place.

2011

U.S. Should Turn To Canada For Energy Needs
Edmonton Journal, January 4, 2011

Why is the price of oil rising, and who is responsible for raising it?

Part of the increase is tied to optimism that the U.S. is on the way back from the most gripping recession since the Dirty Thirties, but mostly it's the wish of the thousands of oil princes who have the power to decide how much of the American recovery the American people can keep and how much will be funneled to the growing wealth of the OPEC suppliers.

So long as Western nations allow themselves to be dependent on unstable, voracious regimes for their energy requirements, they will be victimized.

For the last half century, a major cornerstone of Western foreign policy has been based on the need to keep cheap energy flowing into our factories and cities. Now that Arab oil is no longer cheap, why are we are still trapped into believing that we need it?

Canada has more than enough oil to satisfy North America's needs for years. What is required is an American policy shift. President Obama must stop denigrating Alberta's oil sands and set up joint ventures with Canada to exploit our resources and to break free of OPEC's shackles.

Response: Let go of idea that Canada can meet U.S. energy needs

Len Bennett of Montreal says, "Canada has more than enough oil to satisfy North America's needs for years."

While this is theoretically true, North America (Canada, the U.S. and Mexico) currently consumes about 24 million barrels per day of crude oil, but has a total production of only 15 million bpd, of which Canada supplies just over three million bpd.

In order to make up the shortfall of about nine million bpd -- all of it in the United States -- synthetic crude oil production from Alberta's oilsands, which is presently around 1.5 million bpd, would have to increase by about 600 per cent.

Think of dozens of new extraction plants and upgraders, plus several huge new pipelines. It's not going to happen in the foreseeable future.

Art, Edmonton

ETHICAL OIL
Globe & Mail, January 11, 2011

It would be wonderful if humans could get along without oil, coal or slavery to fuel their economies, but that is wishful thinking (The Oil-Sands Fight Renews). Life would also be better if the world was not so overpopulated that our natural resources were being depleted and that pollution was poisoning us.

Is it better to buy oil from Canada than from OPEC? Is it more ethical to develop oil in democracies, where the population is free, than to purchase fuel from countries that have no concept of human rights?

With every purchase we make, we are voting our approval of the source of the product. We support companies and countries whose attitudes coincide with our own. When we have no choice, we are forced to support dictatorial regimes. So, countries that have no rights for women or gays, that accept honor-killings and that support terrorism are profiting because the developed world is held hostage to resources that we refuse to develop for ourselves.

Comparing Left- Or Right-Wing Speeches To Hitler's Just Plain Wrong
Sun-Sentinel, January 13, 2011

Certainly, violent speech can lead to, or be a precursor to, violence. But equating left- or right-wing Americans' speech to Hitler's, as Democratic Congressman Cohen and your writer have done, is both "vitriolic" and ignorant.

It obfuscates the causes and makes banal the horrors of World War II and the Holocaust that was part of it. Hitler's speeches explained the justification for war and the genocide of the Jews. It was not its cause.

Hitler's attitude towards Jews was commonplace.

From popes to kings, Jews were seen as god-killers. From the misnamed King Richard the Lion Hearted, to the Crusades, to the Inquisition, Jews were slaughtered with the church's encouragement. They were banished, invited back and banished again throughout Europe. They could be robbed by their lords, allowed to rebuild and be robbed again. They were an economic source and a scourge to Christendom.

Hitler's racism was based on centuries of accepted practice. His "vitriolic speeches" followed the norm. They did not create the rationale for the Holocaust.

Organization Shows No Balance
Canadian Jewish News, March 9, 2011

Rabbis for Human Rights is not a human rights organization. They are an advocacy group that supports Palestinian issues and has shown no balance and no regard for the rights of Israelis or Jews.

I particularly found letter writer Leanore Lieblein's condescending comment about the American Jewish Committee and the Anti-Defamation League's "vulnerability on the world stage" to be a nasty backhanded compliment, plainly meant to show that these organizations cannot normally be trusted ("Israeli human rights organizations.")

Well, it is Rabbis for Human Rights itself that cannot be trusted. Israel is indeed "a beacon of democracy" and it's RHR that "is on a witch hunt whose goal is the delegitimization" of that beacon.

BRANDEIS GROUPS CLASH OVER ISRAEL STANCE
Boston Globe, March 15, 2011

Working to cut Israel is an agenda that is unacceptable

In "BRANDEIS groups clash on Israel stance," you report that Hillel is "steadfastly committed to the support of Israel as a Jewish and democratic state with secure and recognized borders as a member of the family of nations." As such, it must reject organizations that "support boycott of, divestment from, or sanctions against the State of Israel." Any organization that works for the elimination of Israel as a Jewish state has an unacceptable agenda.

Democracy, free speech, an independent judiciary, a free press, and an active opposition are essential elements in a liberal democracy. Israel is the only Middle East country that meets these requirements. Israel's Arabs vote, have members in parliament and a Supreme Court judge, and access to Israeli universities and hospitals.

I believe that singling out Israel for massive approbation is symptomatic of bias and anti-Semitism. Hillel at Brandeis University took the appropriate action in refusing to affiliate with the student chapter of Jewish Voice for Peace.

NOBODY KNOWS WHAT THE OUTCOME WILL BE
Wall Street Journal, March 26, 2011

The Arab world is in turmoil and you call it a "democratic tide" ("Upheaval in Mideast Sets Back Terror War.") It is not. It is revolution. Period. There are myriad actors in each situation and no predictable outcomes.

We Are Not Terrorists
Ottawa Citizen, May 11, 2011

Re: Nothing to celebrate.

Overall, I agree there is not much to celebrate in Osama bin Laden's death, except that justice is served and he will not harm anyone again. However, this changes little "for the United States and for the rest of the world."

For letter-writer William Perry to claim that the "execution makes us no better than the terrorists" is grotesque. We will be as bad as the terrorists when we tie suicide belts on our children and women and direct them to blow up crowds of civilians. Till then, we are superior to the terrorists.

Oil
Sun-Sentinel, May 17, 2011

President Obama, like Bush, Clinton and all the other presidents since the 1972 oil crisis, has been negligent. With massive oil reserves left untapped in North America, we are still dependent on the demands of greedy, unstable dictators.

Surely, we should have smartened up by now. The answer is simple. Stop supporting OPEC. Start drilling at home. Alternate sources of energy can be explored once we are energy self-sufficient and have restored our economy.

Unfortunately, so long as Gulf princes pour billions of dollars into lobbying governments and into our universities, pressure to drop OPEC will rarely be heard.

MIDEAST REALITY
National Post, May 18, 2011

Re: *Army Opens Fire As Protesters Cross Border.*

What would the Arabs do if they didn't have Israel to vent their anger at? Tribalism ensures that the vast majority of Arabs remain downtrodden. Children in large, poor families cannot be properly supported — financially or emotionally — to enable them to grow up to be confident, functioning adults. And so they rage, and Israel becomes a handy diversion when they can't address their frustrations more appropriately.

In 1948, 600,000 Palestinian Arabs fled, or were forced out of Israel during the Arabs' failed attempt to "throw the Jews into the sea." 850,000 Jews were forced out of Arab countries and most settled in Israel. The Jews took care of their brothers, but the Arabs treated their kin with disdain. If the Arab nations cared for the Palestinians, they would integrate them and get them off the UN welfare rolls.

U.S. POLICY SHIFT ANGERS ISRAEL
Montreal Gazette, May 20, 2011

President Obama sees the Arab-Israeli conflict from the Arab perspective, and the upheavals throughout the Arab world from a North American point of view.

He portrays the conflicted Arab states' rebellions as if they were NAFTA-like issues. He expects that democracy will produce liberal societies that respect human rights. That works on the New York-Ontario border, but not among the fractious tribes that make up the Arab world. The internecine Arab families and tribes are vying for power. Each hopes to gain control of their self-declared fiefdom, national borders notwithstanding. This is not democracy.

On the Arab-Israeli conflict, the "pre-1967 borders" are not the basis for a peace agreement between Israel and the Palestinians. The base must be the Palestinian acceptance of Israel as a Jewish state and an end to terrorism as a negotiating tool. Then, peace talks hold the prospect of a speedy resolution, and the Palestinians will have the state denied them by the Egyptian and Jordanian occupation of 1948 to 1967.

CANADIAN STANDARD?
Globe & Mail, June 9, 2011

Canadian Arab Federation president Khaled Mouammar (A Principle, Defended) says Canada is "siding unconditionally with Israel." No, it's not. Canada supports Israel because of shared values and the belief that Israel has a right to exist. When the Canadian Arab Federation understands this, it'll be better able to be part of the solution to the Arab-Israeli conflict.

READERS RESPOND TO OUTLOOK ON MIDEAST PEACE
Sun-Sentinel, July 15, 2011

In 1947, the UN voted to partition Palestine into a Jewish state and an Arab (not a Palestinian) state. The Jews accepted the UN decision, and the Arabs did not. Five Arab nations attacked the Jews with the clear intention of slaughtering them. At that time, the Arabs lost any moral right to play the victim. In 1967, with billions of dollars of Soviet weapons, the Arabs again attempted to "drive the Jews into the sea."

The "jig" should be up, but it is not. Where was the U.S. campaign to end the Israeli occupation from 1948 to 1967, when Egypt and Jordan occupied Gaza and the West Bank? Oh yes, the term "Palestinian people" had not been invented yet.

The Palestinian Arabs have refused for 64 years, since the partition of Palestine, to live in freedom and peace alongside Israel. Their commitment to Israel's destruction is the sole reason there is no peace.

ISRAEL FIGHTS BACK
Miami Herald, July 24, 2011

The anti-Israel and anti-Semitic crowds are up in arms. Israel has the nerve to fight back against those trying to destroy it by using the same tactics they use.

The infamous 2001 Durban conference adopted a policy for the isolation of Israel, promoting the falsehood that the only free, democratic Middle East country was an apartheid state. What more grievous claim could be made in South Africa, the country that lived under apartheid? And what more vicious joke could be foisted on the innocent left-wing do-gooders, who rely on sound-bites for their information?

Just as the United States has taken away CAIR's charitable status and Canada has defunded KAIROS, Israel is taking steps to withhold funding and immunity from groups whose function is undemocratic, illegal and often anti-Semitic, and to allow those who have been hurt to seek redress from the courts.

NORWAY: TERROR NOW
Globe & Mail, July 25, 2011

There is no excusing the vicious terror attacks in Norway. Only a seriously perverted mind could conceive of murdering innocent people for the sake of any cause.

The cause in this case is likely Islamic immigration to Europe and the Americas in the past few years.

Electing left or right-wing parliamentarians is a valid and democratic way to induce political change. Resorting to terrorism is not, no matter the perceived injustice.

Why Terrorism Prevails
Miami Herald, August 10, 2011

Why is terrorism the preferred method of getting out a specific point of view? The answer is simple: It works. The more horrendous the act, the more attention is paid by a world inundated with information.

Yasser Arafat hijacked planes, murdered athletes at the Olympics in Germany and blew up buses in Jerusalem and Tel Aviv. Thus he created the Palestinian issue and kept it in the news.

Sept. 11, 2001 was a major victory in the Islamic world. It focused hatred of the decadent Western world and gave hope that it would eventually be replaced by a caliphate.

The Madrid commuter train bombings in 2004 that killed 191 and wounded 1,800 were enough to induce the Spanish government to pull its troops out of Iraq.

The Norway massacres were meant to highlight the problem of Islamic emigration to the West. Most Muslim immigrants don't join the mainstream of their adopted countries, but replicate their cultures and conflicts and aim to establish enclaves where Sharia law overrides the law of the land.

In Britain, for example, the Islamic Emirates Project, launched by Muslims Against Crusades, named Birmingham, Bradford, Derby, Dewsbury, Leeds, Leicester, Liverpool, Luton, Manchester, Sheffield, as well as Waltham Forest in northeast London and Tower Hamlets in East London as territories to be targeted for blanket Sharia rule.

In France, there are over 600 no-go zones, where French police dare not enter, and French citizens are being forced out. In both France and Norway, Jews fear for their safety and are leaving in record numbers.

Will the issue of Islamic immigration now receive more attention and debate in the Western world? If it does, Anders Behring Breivik will have succeeded.

So long as countries cave in to terrorists and the perpetrators see positive results, the scourge will continue.

A Statement Too Far
Globe & Mail, August 23, 2011

Karim Durzi says "the Palestinians played no part in the tragedies that befell the Jews in Europe." I guess he's forgotten about Haj Amin al-Husseini, the Grand Mufti of Jerusalem, who spent the Second World War in Nazi Germany, where he planned the "final solution" of the Jews in the Middle East and recruited Muslims for the Waffen SS.

Apologize, Turkey
Miami Herald, October 7, 2011

The United Nations has concluded that Israel's naval blockade is in keeping with international law and that its forces have the right to stop Gaza-bound ships in international waters.

It is now time for Turkey to apologize to Israel and the world for encouraging the illegal flotilla, which included Humanitarian Relief Foundation (IHH) terrorists that tried to break the blockade.

Statehood Would Jeopardize Relationships
Sun-Sentinel, October 25, 2011

The Palestinian territories hardly satisfy all the requirements for statehood. Palestine is a welfare state, relying on the charity of the United States and Israel for its survival. Like South Sudan, it can develop, so long as the World Bank, the International Monetary Fund, the EU, the United States and Israel are willing to carry it. Its precipitous, unilateral move for U.N. statehood could jeopardize these relationships.

Israel's occupation of the West Bank and Gaza was the result of the Arab wars to "drive the Jews into the sea." The separation barrier was installed because Yasser Arafat sent Palestinian terrorists to blow up innocent Israeli civilians on buses and in restaurants and hotels.

No objective minds would presume that Israeli activities inevitably change the status of the territory. Israel removed settlements from Sinai in return for peace with Egypt. Israel removed settlements from Gaza, hoping for peace, but got terror instead.

The 64-year delay in Arab/Palestinian statehood was caused by the Arab states and continues by their refusal to accept an infidel state in their midst. Lebanon is an example of how Islamic persistence paid off. Sovereign states have the right to use reasonable force to defend their territorial integrity and citizens, as the U.N. report on Israel's legal blockade of Gaza has reaffirmed.

The U.N., with its historic anti-democratic and anti-Semitic bias, will certainly get 120 countries to support Palestinian statehood. However, the Palestinians, like the occupied Gazans and Lebanese, may suffer from that success.

THE SCHALIT DEBATE
Jerusalem Post, October 28, 2011

Readers express their views on the prisoner exchange.

Sir—What a sad spectacle the world has witnessed in the past few days.

One emaciated, sunlight deprived Israeli soldier, held in mind-numbing isolation for 5 years and 4 months, was traded for 1027 well-fed, humanely treated Palestinian convicts.

Gilad Schalit was kidnapped by Hamas terrorists in a cross-border raid when he was 19 years old. He is now 25. The Red Cross, Doctors without Borders and the other NGOs who continued to work in Gaza, while being barred from access to Gilad, should hang their heads in shame.

The Palestinian prisoners had all the access they needed to food, Korans, exercise and the essentials that civility demands, watched over by these same NGOs. The prisoners include terrorists who murdered Israeli, American and other civilians in restaurants, clubs, hotels, universities, and on busses. There were also likely common criminals and fathers and brothers who murdered their daughters and sisters in honor-killings. All returned home as heroes. Palestinian President Abbas even referred to them as "freedom fighters."

When will we realize that not all cultures are equal? When will the West hold the Islamic world to at least a minimum standard?

GINGRICH SPOKE TRUTH ABOUT PALESTINIANS
Sun-Sentinel, December 12, 2011

Newt Gingrich told the truth and the Arabs and the politically correct left-wing, including some Republicans, respond as expected.

The "ignorant, provocative and racist nature" of the Fatah remarks are typical, and reflect the historical revisionism they promote.

The reality is that Arabs, mostly from Egypt and Syria followed the Jewish migration to Palestine in search of jobs.

Half the Arab of Palestine in 1948 were these immigrants. The Palestinian Arabs always considered themselves to be part of the greater Arab nation. With the establishment of Israel, the Arab League promoted the ethnic cleansing of Jews in Arab lands and 850,000 were forced out of their homes. Most fled, penniless, to Israel.

After three wars of genocide against Israel in 1948, 1967 and 1973, the Egyptians had enough. They would no longer waste blood and treasure fighting to destroying Israel.

With the military option gone, the psychological, political war began. The Arabs of Palestine were now rebranded as "Palestinians" and a world-wide campaign to disenfranchise Israel was launched.

After the Oslo Accords, when the PLO was given most of Gaza and the West Bank to start state-building, Arafat claimed there was no Jewish attachment to Israel. Everything Jewish was re-labeled as Palestinian. Jewish holy sites were turned into mosques.

The lies continue with the financial support of the oil states and the political support of the Arab-dominated United Nations.

Hopefully, Gingrich has cast a light into the dark shadows of casual left-wing anti-Semitism, and an honest dialogue on the Arab-Israeli conflict can begin.

2012

The High Stakes In The Israel-Iran Conflict
Washington Post, February 18, 2012

Fareed Zakaria reached back to 1914 Europe and then leapfrogged past World War II to give examples of failed and successful military action. How does he manage to ignore the 1930s, World War II and the Holocaust? He is discussing the state of Israel, the homeland of the Jews. How does he ignore the major cataclysm of the 20th century, which saw the murder of one of every three Jews in the world?

How does he not compare the words of Iranian President Mahmoud Ahmadinejad to those of Adolf Hitler? That's the realistic reference from which to consider Israeli military action against Iran. Israel is, in fact, confronting the sort of choices the United States and Britain confronted in the 1930s. One hopes Israel will be wiser than they were.

What Does The West Do About Iran?
National Post, February 27, 2012

Israel is key to any solution

The West should, but will not, attack Iran's nuclear facilities. It will be left to Israel because it is facing the perfect storm. The United States and the European Union have as much to lose as Israel has, but their governments are content to have Israel do their dirty work for them. Unless. Europe and the United States take dramatic steps, Israel will be at risk.

REPUBLICANS, NOT OBAMA, RIGHT
ABOUT CONFRONTING IRAN
Sun-Sentinel, March 7, 2012

"Hope is not a foreign policy," Mitt Romney said.

The Obama administration is not convinced Iran's leaders have decided to develop a weapon. Do they refuse to listen, or believe, what the Iranian leadership has been saying, namely, that they will wipe Israel off the map?

Iran will use "talks to buy time." They care little for what the U.S. or E.U. think. They have focus and a mission, while the West procrastinates.

Mr. Obama warned his Republican opponents "about launching a military attack on Iran's nuclear facilities." In 1938, Neville Chamberlain warned of the consequences of an attack against Germany, promising 'peace in our time.'

The president's Muslim advisors all have ties to the Muslin Brotherhood, and though the main-stream media paints them as moderates, the Brotherhood still controls Sunni terrorism world-wide. From oil blackmail to the multi-billion dollar subjugation of our universities' Middle East departments, Arab influence has polluted American foreign policy.

Obama courted Netanyahu this week in an attempt to sway the Jewish vote in one or two swing ridings that could impact the 2012 election. He has little need for Jewish funding, as the Saudis and Georges Soros will ensure his war chest is flush.

Obama may agree to 'red lines' against Iran, but he will act on the suggestions of his M.E. Muslim advisors, as he has done throughout the Arab Spring that ousted America's partners in favor of radical religious regimes.

NY OFFICIALS DOING THEIR JOB
March 18, 2012, Sun Sentinel

Kudos to Mayor Michael Bloomberg, Commissioner Raymond Kelly and the people of New York for doing their job, which is ensuring the safety of their city.

The purpose of surveillance is intelligence gathering, something that was tragically lacking before Sept. 11.

The surveillance of law-abiding Muslims in New York City, Long Island, and New Jersey is functionally necessary to allow law enforcement to develop link-analysis of suspected and potential criminal or terrorist activity.

The politically-correct, knee-jerk reaction of many Muslim public figures and leaders of universities is understandable. Mosques and universities are hotbeds of anti-American, anti-infidel activism.

Many American mosques are Saudi-funded, as are many of our universities' Middle East programs. Their teachings reflect the Wahhabism of their benefactors and breeds radicalism.

While not all Muslims are potential radicals, some are, and their social, business and criminal activities will form patterns that law enforcement could analyze to monitor and prevent violence, criminal activities and terrorism.

The public is the eyes and ears of civil society. Muslims, like other citizens, should cooperate with the authorities and welcome the opportunity to cleanse their communities of those who would harm us all.

ARE YOU READY TO WELCOME BACK KHADR?
National Post, May 1, 2012

No, Khadr is not welcome in Canada. Not because he isn't white, as some writers claim, but because he is an unrepentant Islamic terrorist and a murderer. He hates infidels and democracy. If he was white, I doubt there'd be this pressure to repatriate him.

IRAN NO THREAT?
Canadian Jewish News, May 17, 2012

How unfortunate that David Tal holds the Kahanoff Chair of Israeli Studies at the University of Calgary and will be molding impressionable graduate students with his faulty, hostile, anti-Israel version of Middle Eastern history

("Iran no real threat, Israeli historian says.") To say that "Iran is not an aggressive state. It has never attacked its enemies first," ignores the Iranian/Hezbollah bombing of the Israeli Embassy and the Jewish community center (AMIA) in Buenos Aires in 1992 and its recent attacks on Israeli embassy employees in New Delhi, India, and Tbilisi, Georgia.

THE ISSUE: WHETHER THE UNITED STATES SHOULD ACT TO STOP THE SYRIAN REGIME'S ATROCITIES.
New York Post, June 2, 2012

President Obama is correctly "reading polls that show little public appetite for new Mideast engagement," as Benny Avni writes.

Even the Arabs do not care if other Arabs are murdered unless it fits into their feudal model.

The so-called "Arab Spring" has seen cruel, somewhat secular dictatorships replaced by equally violent Islamist dictatorships.

The Arabs are rightly suspicious when Americans interfere.

OPPONENTS OF ISRAEL WOULD PREFER VIOLENT ARAB STATE
Sun-Sentinel, June 5, 2012

Students for Justice in Palestine must also advocate for Israel's right to live in peace and security alongside an independent Palestine. If they do not, they are advocating genocide against the only modern, successful, liberal democracy in the Middle East.

Those who support "the Israel boycott, divestment and sanctions movement" attest to their desire to delegitimize Israel and replace it with another backward, violent Arab state. As darkness descends over the 'Arab spring,' surely, even hard-core racists cannot still blame Israel for all the Middle East's death and destruction.

Church Report Not 'Balanced'
Canadian Jewish News, July 26, 2012

There is nothing fairly "balanced" about the United Church's report. The fact that the church would even consider studying the boycotting of Israel while ignoring all of the rest of the Middle East is blatant anti-Semitism ("The United Church report.")

There is only one reason to single out Israel. The reason is the desire to deny the Jewish People a homeland. As for Peter Beinart's book, The Crisis of Zionism, it is misnamed. It should be called "The Crisis in Anti-Zionism." There is no crisis among mainstream Jews. The crisis is among fringe groups and shtetl Jews who believe we have to keep quiet and be nice to our oppressors in the hope they'll go easy on us. It didn't work in 1938, and it won't work now.

Sham And shame
Calgary Herald, September 1, 2012

Re: Dismissive.

I am dismayed that Rev. R.W. Mutlow can so easily dismiss the genuine concerns raised by those outraged by the United Church's obvious anti-Semitism. To say a word of truth is to recognize that Christians are being persecuted everywhere in the Middle East, except in Israel, where they are thriving and growing in numbers.

I understand that to not criticize Israel is to exacerbate the problems faced by non-Muslims in the region, but to join in Jew-baiting is a worse action.

The United Church of Canada will not soon outlive this sham or this shame.

NAIVE ADMINISTRATION
Miami Herald, October 12, 2012

The chickens are coming home to roost.

This administration naively thought they could interfere in multi-faction insurrections in the Arab world without consequences.

In the fractious family against family, tribe against tribe, religion against religion world of the Middle East, we have no place taking sides, hoping to pick a winner and gain influence.

In Libya we bombed. In Egypt, we threw out our closest Arab ally. Our reward has been two radical Islamist governments and our embassies under attack.

The outcome of our meddling is our friends don't trust us and our enemies don't fear us. Will we be surprised if Israel feels compelled to act alone against Iran?

THE UNITED CHURCH WAS WRONG
Montreal Gazette, October 28, 2012

Re: *Boycott is not a question of Israel's right to exist.*

"The debate" related to the United Church of Canada was an emotional collection of shallow misinterpretations of the Fourth Geneva Conventions, Article 49, which I doubt any of the contributors, or the UCC actually read.

Article 49 states: "Individual or mass forcible transfer, as well as deportations of protected persons from occupied territory to the territory of the Occupying Power or to that of any other country, occupied or not, are prohibited, regardless of their motives."

It also says: "The Occupying Power shall not deport or transfer parts of its own civilian population into the territory it occupies."

Article 49 is about forced transfer of civilian populations. There have been no forced population transfers into or out of the West Bank.

Examples of forced transfers would be the Nazis and their collaborators' deportations during the Second World War, the allies' transfer of Germans after the Second World War, and the Arab states' eviction of Jews after 1948.

The boycott is "a question of Israel's right to exist." In 1948, 1967 and 1973, Israel's Arab neighbors made it perfectly clear their goal was genocide and the Jews would be driven into the sea. Israel occupies the West Bank today as a consequence of illegal Arab actions.

Just as the allies occupied Germany and Japan after the Second World War, Israel has the legal right to occupy captured territory until a peace treaty is signed dictating otherwise.

How Do We Identify Who Truly Is An Anti-Semite?
National Post, November 7, 2012

The most common reason to hate Israel is still anti-Semitism. So who is clearly anti-Semitic and not merely critical of this or that Israeli action? The United Nations is blatantly anti-Semitic in its persistent negative focus on Israel to the exclusion of the violent human rights abusers surrounding her. Islamic groups, such as the Muslim Brotherhood and their progeny — such as the Israel Apartheid Week and Boycott, Divest and Sanction groups that pollute our universities — clearly are passionately anti-Semitic. Terrorists like Hamas, Hezbollah, Fatah and their fellow-travelers like the Gaza flotilla folks are racists as well.

There are also numerous fringe Jewish groups bent on bringing Israel to its knees. That includes organizations such B'Tselem, J-Street and Peace Now, whose goal is not to support Israel, but to make Israel more acceptable to their left-wing, progressive ideologies. If some of these groups are not anti-Semitic, they are at best useful idiots.

WHAT THE ISRAELIS AND GAZANS ARE FIGHTING FOR
Los Angeles Times, November 22, 2012

Israel has not "embraced a theory of 'deterrence' with respect to the Gaza Strip."

Israel occupied the Gaza Strip in 1967 after the Arabs failed to drive the Jews into the sea. In 2005, Israel left Gaza as a goodwill gesture. Given the opportunity to develop their own unique society, the Gazans instead engaged in a civil war, with Hamas against Fatah. Then they launched a terror campaign against Israel.

Older Palestinians and Israelis remember the good times, between 1967 and 1993, when everyone crossed back and forth between Gaza, Israel and the West Bank to work, shop and play. Then came the Oslo Accords, Yasser Arafat and terrorism.

The Palestinians are the source of their own accomplishments and troubles, aided by the Arab League and the United Nations, which holds them as welfare clients.

COMMENTS: Len Bennett, you got it exactly right. *Abe*

MIDDLE EASTERN STABILITY THREATENED
USA Today, November 23, 2012

Why should anyone be surprised Israel struck a blow at Hamas headquarters to undermine its infrastructure? Hamas had fired hundreds of rockets into Israeli civilian areas in 2012 and should have expected retaliatory raids. The West understands that Israel will attack targets serving as bases for terror against Israel.

As for Mahmoud Abbas' outrage, he depends on American welfare to survive and is happy to see his rival, Hamas, taken down a notch. Egypt's new Islamist President Mohammed Morsi is also beholden to the U.S. The Arab League has enough to do without worrying about Hamas Prime Minister Ismail Haniyeh.

Canada And The Palestinians
Montreal Gazette, December 1, 2012

Re: Canada's UN vote on Palestinians was shameful.

Canadians proudly voted based on our values and did not meekly follow the mob.

Given the chance to make a statement, the UN will always go with the dictatorship against the democracy, the tyrant against freedom. There is no concept of right and wrong. There is only the need for the self-preservation of each ruling family, for that is what makes up the majority of UN member states.

That the villain today is Israel, confronted by the Arab League and a UN that has kept Palestinian Arabs as hostages for so many years, boggles the thinking mind.

The message the UN is sending is that the short-lived experiment of liberal democracy is coming to an end. So long as the despots can outvote the democracies and the democracies, fed by guilt perhaps, accept this, our free societies are at risk.

Israel is a tiny, easy target. The West, controlled by liberal progressives, will not wake up until it is too late to save the freedom we pretend to cherish.

Rebuttal:

Len Bennett's letter to the editor reads as if it were sent from an alternate universe. How else to explain his contention that the UN vote to recognize Palestine as a non-voting observer state represents an example of the "despots" outvoting the "democracies"? The only states to vote against the resolution were Israel, the United States, Canada, the Czech Republic, the Marshall Islands, Micronesia, Nauru, Palau and Panama. The vast majority of democracies, western or otherwise, voted in favor of the resolution.

Likewise, The Gazette's editorial of the same date suggests that Canada's vote was merely in favor of a negotiated settlement, ignoring the fact that most international observers cite Israeli refusal to halt settlement construction in the occupied territories as the prime roadblock to negotiations. One need search no further than Israeli newspaper Ha'aretz to find that many, if not most, Israeli pundits do not believe that Israel, particularly under the belligerent governance of Benjamin Netanyahu, has any interest in a negotiated peace.

Our Conservative government's unconditional support for an illegal Israeli occupation that has gone on for nearly 50 years is a black mark on our international reputation, one which will not be looked upon kindly by the history books of years to come.

ETHAN COX, MONTREAL
PALESTINIANS—NO STATE FOR YOU
National Post, December 3, 2012

Palestinians should have a state when Hamas, Fatah and the Arab League abandon genocidal barbarism against Israel and accept the Jewish homeland.

When Palestinians love their children enough to reject terrorists and imams who teach them to hate Infidels and to kill themselves for Allah, they will be more worthy of peoplehood.

If Palestinians are willing to have a country that includes Jews and gays, living in peace alongside Israel, I support them.

IT'S NOT UP TO ISRAEL
Calgary Herald, December 17, 2012

Re: Many Israelis believe Palestinians don't want peace.

Barbara Yaffe has clearly portrayed the state of Arab-Israeli relations. After the Palestinians went to the Jew-hating UN, why should it be Israel's responsibility to persuade them to come back to talks?

Did Canada and her allies beg Germany to talk to them in 1945? No. They firebombed it into submission, divided the country in four sections, occupied it and hanged its leaders.

That's how Canada reacted after fighting German aggression twice in a 30-year period. Why should Israel's response be different? Israel defended itself from Arab attempted genocide three times since 1948. Is Israel that morally superior to Canada, or has it foolishly ignored the lessons of the Second World War?

PLO/Fatah has broken every agreement that allowed them into Ramallah to establish a Palestinian state living in peace alongside Israel. They have never eschewed terrorism and propaganda to discredit Israel and to drive the Jews from Israel, as their brothers throughout the Arab world have done in their countries.

Until free nations stop groveling to the Arab League and demand a return to peace talks, the plan for a two-state solution will remain a pipe dream.

The Arabs could have created Palestine from 1948 to 1967, but they had no wish to. They can restart the process any time, or they can let the Palestinian refugees fester in neighboring countries.

Benjamin Netanyahu does not need to keep proposing the Palestinians sit down with him. He should wait until they become interested. Meanwhile, he has a country to protect and develop.

"There is only one way to avoid criticism: do nothing, say nothing, and be nothing." —Aristotle

_____

2013

GERALD SCARFE'S CARICATURE
Sunday Times (London), February 2, 2013

It was with disgust and disbelief I saw Gerald Scarfe's caricature of Israeli Prime Minister Netanyahu.

Is your racist depiction a rejection of Israel's democracy? Would you dare depict any Arab leader in such a way without expecting a violent response?

It is little wonder that Jews are fleeing Britain? Is it any wonder that Islamic no-go zones are expanding throughout your pathetic island?

Remember, after they come for the Jews, they'll come for the Christians and other infidels.

You are a disgrace to journalism.

Response:

Dear Mr. Bennett,

I am grateful to you for writing to *The Sunday Times* and expressing your views so clearly. I'd like to apologize at the outset for the offence caused by Gerald Scarfe's cartoon published last Sunday.

Its publication was a terrible mistake. The timing – on Holocaust Memorial Day - was inexcusable. The associations on this occasion were grotesque. As someone who understands the history and iconography in this context, I appreciate fully why publication has caused such offence and I apologize unreservedly for my part in that.

I sought an urgent meeting with leading members of the Jewish community, and am pleased to say that we got together on Tuesday evening. It was a frank but constructive meeting. Mick Davis, Chair of the Jewish Leadership Council, accepted my apology on behalf of the group and told the press afterwards that the community "now looks forward to constructively moving on from this affair".

I hope you will find this reply reassuring, I thank you again for your correspondence.

Yours sincerely,

Martin Ivens, Acting Editor

HAGEL'S DUBIOUS FUTURE: WILL GOP BLOCK O'S PICK?
New York Post, February 19, 2013

Hagel's nomination for secretary of defense and Schumer's support of him are part of the new progressive left's casual anti-Semitism ("New Hagel Horrors," John Podhoretz, Post Opinion.)

It should make Americans up-chuck.

ISRAEL IS VULNERABLE
Miami Herald, March 21, 2013

President Obama has a surprising lack of understanding of the key hurdles to having two states for two people. To Israelis, it means a Jewish state living side by side in peace and security with a Palestinian Arab state. From the Palestinian perspective, Israel should be a multi-ethnic state to which any refugees and their descendants could move, thus ending the Jewish majority and character of Israel.

Border swaps is another point of contention. Under the Clinton formula, the land swap was based on area. To Fatah, it's based on the value. Both consider Jerusalem to be invaluable. Other impediments are Hamas' pledge to destroy Israel, Fatah's acquiescence to their rival's ideas, the Muslim Brotherhood's ascendancy in the Middle East and the Arab belief that Obama's is the most Islamic-friendly administration in history.

Unless Obama can move the Arabs closer to the Clinton plan and thwart the Iranian nuclear bomb, Israel is vulnerable.

OBAMA'S MIDEAST MEDDLING: AN UNDESERVED APOLOGY
New York Post, March 26, 2013

No wonder we are skeptical about politicians.

Obama convinced Israel and Turkey to bury the hatchet. The Islamist-run state, dependent on saving face, got a phony apology from Israel.

It is undeniable the ship, the MV Mavi Marmara, had terrorists aboard who attacked the Israeli soldiers before they were subdued.

The United Nations stated the blockade was legal. Turkey supported and promoted the illegal flotilla.

So what did Obama promise Turkey and Israel to get them to go through with this charade?

UNTYING THE MIDDLE EAST KNOT
Los Angeles Times, March 29, 2013

With President Obama's visit to the Mideast behind us, it is hoped the Palestinians can overcome their internal politics and pursue peace.

The Palestinians have demonstrated the maxim of one man, one vote, one time. Sectarian rivalries make democracy impossible; only compromise among ruling factions provides any stability. The regimes that surround Israel are changed by the sword, not the ballot box.

Palestinians are indeed frustrated, living so close and yet so far from the modern miracle that is Israel. If their leaders forswore anti-Semitism and took up the challenge, there would quickly be a Palestine linked economy with Israel that would be the envy of its less-advanced neighbors.

"International acceptance and domestic legitimacy" for Palestine depend on peace with Israel. America recognizes this; so should the Palestinians.

Israel Is The Only Liberal Democracy In The Middle East
Montreal Gazette, April 25, 2013

Re: Israel and democracy.

Where can I start to refute the misinformation Ziad Aki has described?

The simple reality is that Israel is the only liberal democracy in the Middle East.

Arab gays find safety from imprisonment and death in Israel. Bedouin forced out of Gaza have set up illegal settlements in Israel's Negev region. Only in Israel is the Christian population growing. Arab parties and members are in parliament and an Arab sits on the Supreme Court. This represents democracy, freedom and diversity.

There are some restrictions for Arabs and ultra-orthodox Jews who don't serve in the military or do other national service, but all are free to volunteer. Arabs and Israelis attend the same universities and hospitals, and many other Arabs are treated in Israeli hospitals as well.

The Palestinian Authority is responsible for the daily lives of most West Bank Arabs. There are no Jewish roads. There are separate roads for Israeli license plates to avoid Arab towns and attacks on civilian traffic.

The UN has passed no laws to prevent suicide bombers from blowing themselves up in Sbarro's Pizza, the cafeteria of Hebrew University, as well as on civilian buses, beaches, clubs and hotels.

Israeli Arabs live better than any other Arabs, and are certainly better integrated into society than those in Europe. The Palestinians could participate in the modernity that peace with Israel would provide.

Syria Used As Conduit To
Illegally Arm Hezbollah
Washington Examiner, May 10, 2013

Re: Obama's blink on Syria could bring peril to allies.

Israel's recent attacks against the advanced weapons Syria is trying to ship to Hezbollah have brought a level of clarity to the Middle East conundrum that heretofore has been missing.

With the exception of Syria, the Arab League hates Iran and is desperate to foil its plan to dominate the Organization of Islamic Cooperation. They support the overthrow of the Assad regime and are secretly applauding Israel's attacks while feigning the expected outrage against "Israel's aggression."

The Arabs are happy to have Hezbollah and Hamas continue to amass weapons, primarily destined for attacking Israel, and will deal with their subservience to Iran in due time.

Iran is outraged. They have Bashar Assad's Syria as an ally and a conduit for illegally arming Hezbollah in defiance of U.N. Security Council Resolution 1701, which ended the 2006 Israel-Hezbollah war and stipulated the disarmament of Hezbollah.

The oil princes fear the Muslim Brotherhood and the myriad armed factions threatening their kingdoms, and everyone hates the Jews, the old whipping boy they drag out to distract their people from the misery of life under medieval Islamic regimes.

Why Qatar Is Seeking Aviation Hub
Toronto Star, May 11, 2013

Once again we have the spectacle of an Arab dictator threatening a liberal democracy. And once again we have the media searching for anything to excuse the bad behavior of an oil-rich bully. This time it's because Canada supports the only Middle East country with which it shares common values.

Qatar, of course, has the "rabid" backing of the anti-Semitic Organization for Islamic Co-operation. With Qatar's financial prowess, it should build decent housing in the so-called refugee camps spread around the Arab world. Or is its concern for Palestinians only a facade?

SINGLING OUT ISRAEL SMACKS OF DESIRE TO DENY JEWS A HOMELAND
Boston Globe, May 14, 2013

It was with disgust that I read of Stephen Hawking's decision to boycott a conference in Israel. Thousands of black Africans, including Christians, are slaves to Muslims in Mauritania, Sudan, Saudi Arabia, and elsewhere, but there appear to be no calls for a boycott, divestment, and sanctions movement against them. The way I see it, there is only one reason to single out Israel, and it is the desire to deny the Jewish people a homeland. The outrageous resolution for a comprehensive boycott is opposed by anyone interested in an independent Palestinian state living in peace and security alongside Israel.

With Islamist clans ripping each other apart throughout the Middle East, settlements are a minor impediment in the region. The intractable problem is Islamic rejection of Jews, Christians, Hindus, and others throughout the world and the so-called useful idiots, like Hawking, who pacify them.

WHAT TO DO ABOUT SYRIA? STAY FAR AWAY FROM IT
New York Post, May 24, 2013

Americans have to ask the right questions to understand our role in the Middle East.

The facts point to the Obama administration relying on only one source of input for all its decisions regarding the Middle East and the Islamic world: its own Muslim members.

From supporting the overthrow of secular dictators in the Middle East, to cleansing FBI and CIA training manuals of all references to radical Islam, to supporting UN legislation making criticism of Islam a crime, this administration has taken positions supporting the Muslim Brotherhood's agenda.

To prevent another Benghazi, the president needs to excise those who support the group from his administration and bring in advisers with values akin to the freedoms Americans cherish.

THE REAL REASONS BEHIND BOYCOTTS
National Post, June 12, 2013

Re: How Boycotts Hurt The Cause Of Peace In The Middle East.

Abraham Cooper and Yitzchok Adlerstein make some good points, but they miss the key element behind the boycott, divest and sanction (BDS) movement. No amount of trying to explain how wonderful Israel is in comparison to its neighbors will convince the country's detractors or have any real effect on the Arab-Israeli conflict.

Just as Queers Against Israeli Apartheid hate Israel—the only gay-friendly country in the Middle East—and the United Church of Canada ignores slavery in Saudi Arabia and Sudan, anti-Semitism overrules self-interest. While gays are murdered in Gaza and Christians are enslaved, or are being forced out of Arab countries, these racists give the jihadists a pass.

All these groups, which are so popular with the left, have little effect on events. Israel has diplomatic ties with most of the world. Its economic growth, scientific achievements and literary output exceeds every country other than the U.S. Its thriving and diverse democracy sticks in the craw of every dictator.

So let them hold their little rallies and write libelous resolutions. The real world is ignoring them.

MIDEAST 'APARTHEID'
Miami Herald, July 8, 2013

The June 25 story *Arab Idol champ in Gaza, urges Palestinian unity* illustrates the frustrations and insecurity Palestinian refugees endure under their fractious and duplicitous leadership. But they do not go far enough.

Why is a talented young man like Mohammed Assaf, the new Arab Idol, and his family still living in a refugee camp?

The 1948 Arab-Israeli war displaced thousands of Arabs and Jews. Jewish refugees found haven in Israel and elsewhere, but the United Nations set up a special agency, the United Nations Relief and Works Agency, to care for the Arab refugees.

Egypt and Jordan occupied Gaza and the West Bank. Jordan offered citizenship to everyone, and UNRWA offered refugee status to anyone who claimed to have lived in Israel for two years. West Bank Arabs chose whether to accept Jordanian citizenship, UN refugee status or to remain Palestinian Arabs.

Today, there are two distinct classes of Palestinians: those who are free and live in towns and cities and those who are refugees.

The refugees are forced to live in camps and are not allowed to move out. They survive on welfare, have restricted employment opportunities and little control over their lives. Palestinian refugees in Gaza and the West Bank live no better than those in Lebanon, Syria and Jordan, even though they are governed by their own people.

UNRWA, with the collaboration of the Arab League, has created a system of Palestinian apartheid.

ARAB UPRISINGS ARE NOT ABOUT DEMOCRACY
Gulf Daily News, Bahrain, August 5, 2013

The Arab world is in turmoil and some still call it a democratic movement. It is not. It is revolution, period.

There are myriad actors in each situation and no predictable outcomes.

The Arab world is not made up of countries.

The countries are just squiggles on a map made by the victors following the collapse of the Ottoman Empire (1299-1923).

In the Arab world, loyalty is to the family first and then to the tribe.

There is the complication of Sunni, Shi'ite and other subsets of Islam. Some work with whoever is in charge, like the Druze.

Many residents are persecuted, like the Baha'i, the Christians, the Bedouin and the Roma.

The big winner is Iran, which is Persian, not Arab. Iran has proxies in Gaza and Lebanon and friends in Syria.

A common factor in this unrest is the Muslim Brotherhood, the only organized political party whose influence is felt globally.

Its goal, since its inception in 1928 by Hassan Al Banna, has been Islamic world domination.

Many senior positions in the Obama administration are filled by associates of the Brotherhood and it influences how many governments react in their Middle East policies.

But the last thing foreigners should do is focus their efforts and share responsibility with this or that Arab entity.

They will not influence which factions will ultimately attain victory and will certainly not promote democracy.

ISRAEL'S FUTURE AS A JEWISH STATE
Los Angeles Time, August 14, 2013

The Times raises the question of whether Israel can be both a democratic and a Jewish state.

Since 1948, Israel has always been Jewish and democratic and will remain so. Every Israeli Arab has the same rights as anyone else. They vote, have political parties and have members in the Knesset. They go to the same universities and hospitals as all residents do.

Israeli Arabs are among the most-well-off Arabs in the world, having been saved from the less fortunate lives of their brothers across the Middle East. They are included in the literate, scientific and democratic society that is Israel.

DOUBLE STANDARD RACIST
Calgary Herald, August 21, 2013

Re: Biased.

I don't speak for Honest Reporting, but I assume their function is to correct erroneous, racist and biased articles written about Israel in the media. Letters such as Barry Jones's demand a response.

Israel has never been charged with "war crimes." There is no "illegal occupation." According to UN resolutions 242 and 338, the borders between Israel and Arab Palestine will be determined by the parties, and this has not yet happened, so legally, the territories are disputed, not occupied.

The UN has declared Israel's Gaza military blockade to be legal. Israel's security barrier was constructed in response to Palestinian terrorism. Inconvenienced Arabs can blame their own leaders.

The Haganah, Irgun and Stern gangs were local militias formed to protect farms from marauding Arabs. Later, they fought the British. The British violated their mandate and the League of Nations mandate by blocking Jews from fleeing the Nazis. The Brits supported the Arabs and hanged Jews who fought them and smuggled in refugees.

Israel does not exist because of "American financial and military support." Israel is a thriving, diverse, democratic country. Its scientific, medical and literary accomplishments and output are superior to every nation on Earth, except for the U.S., and no American soldier has ever had so much as a nosebleed defending Israel.

Criticizing Israel is as legitimate as criticizing Canada. Gross exaggeration and double standards smack of racism.

EGYPT IN FLAMES
Toronto Star, August 24, 2013

Is there an axis of evil in Washington that rejects traditional Western values? Why is the Muslim Brotherhood guiding Obama and the Clintons in determining U.S. foreign policy?

Arif Alikhan, Mohammed Elibiary, Rashad Hussain, Salam al-

Marayati, Imam Mohamed Magid, Eboo Patel, Huma Abedin and John Brennan hold senior positions in the administration. All are closely associated with the Brotherhood and are the only Muslim opinions heard in the White House.

From helping overthrow secular regimes in Libya and Egypt and replacing them with radical Brotherhood/Al Qaeda Islamists, America has lost any respect or influence it used to have in the Middle East. An American ambassador raped and murdered in Libya and Christians being slaughtered and their churches burned in Egypt are the legacies of the U.S. siding with the Sunni terrorist Muslim Brotherhood.

From cleansing FBI and CIA training manuals of references to radical Islam, to supporting UN resolutions making criticism of Islam a crime, to forcing Israel to release Palestinian terrorists, to pushing for Morsi's return in Egypt, this bumbling administration is proving that bullying its friends and pandering to the Brotherhood is their agenda.

It is little wonder the U.S. is neither feared nor admired any more. It's time to cut ties with the Muslim Brotherhood. They have destroyed America's credibility.

Quebec 'Values' Fight May Backfire
Calgary Herald, September 14, 2013

If Quebec Premier Pauline Marois and her supporters were being more honest with themselves, they would admit they are afraid of Islam and worried Quebec society would go the way of Europe.

After 9/11, Western democracies bent over backwards to demonstrate they were not anti-Islam. Our federal government went overboard, focusing funding in the Muslim community to the exclusion of other ethnic groups.

We have had massive immigration in the past few years, even though it is a net loss to Canada of $30 billion annually, according to the Fraser Institute. Twenty five per cent of our immigration is from Islamic countries.

In Europe, Islamic immigration has fractured traditional society. Finland is now considered the most anti-Semitic country in Europe. One Muslim imam referred to Sweden as the best Muslim country in the world.

Martin Schultz, president of the European Parliament, recently stated, "Jewish people are living in fear in Europe."

Europe is pockmarked with no-go zones, where sharia law is the only law and natives have been forced out. It appears Mme. Marois is trying to prevent Quebec from being overwhelmed by people whose values are inimical to hers and Quebec society.

CONFESSION APP CAN'T MAKE THINGS RIGHT
Wall Street Journal, September 24, 2013

I am offended by Rebecca Meiser's flippant characterization of Yom Kippur ("Atoning for Yom Kippur—There's an App for That," Houses of Worship.)

Jews don't just confess their sins. If one has sinned against his fellow man, he is obligated to ask forgiveness of that person and to make restitution to that person before Rosh Hashana, the Jewish New Year. If he does not, he is approaching the Days of Awe with the sin still on him.

On Yom Kippur, a believer asks God to forgive the sins he has made against God, be they intentional or accidental, and hopes to be inscribed in the book of life for the coming year.

In this age of computer games, eScapegoat is only that.

ARAFAT WRECKED OSLO
Canadian Jewish News, October 2, 2013

Any objective observer would say the Oslo peace accords were wrecked in 2000 by then-Palestinian Authority president Yasser Arafat ("Twenty years later, debate on Oslo accords rages.")

At the Camp David talks between then-U.S. President Bill Clinton, then-Israeli prime minister Ehud Barak and Arafat, the Palestinians were to get all of Gaza, 97 per cent of the West Bank (with an equivalent swap of Israeli land) and their capital in a shared Jerusalem. It was everything anyone could have dreamed of. But Arafat refused to sign, and he wouldn't make a counter-proposal. The problem was an "end-of-conflict" statement, which would not have left it open for future generations to finally "drive the Jews into the sea."

So, when he should have been building his new state, Arafat started the second intifada, unleashing suicide bombers on innocent Israeli civilians in hotels, restaurants, universities and buses.

Now, as the two sides are again starting talks, we will soon see who is honorable and who is not. Hopefully, both sides will prove equal to the task.

ASSESSING IRAN'S CHARM OFFENSIVE
Toronto Star, October 5, 2013

"Moves by the U.S. and Iran" prove the U.S. is like the desperate high school girl who finally got to speak to the quarterback. What is the UN, who are its members and is it worth the time and energy the West pours into it? All in all, the United Nations is a conduit for the developed world to pump billions of dollars into the coffers of kings and dictators.

Few member countries are liberal democracies. Most are feudal dictatorships, led by the 57 members of the Islamic block, whose votes and oil dictate the agenda of the UN General Assembly. They are anti-Western, anti-democratic and anti-Infidel, with a special animus for Jews.

The representatives of these dictatorships are invariably related to the ruler, as they are in all international fora.

Diplomatically, the UN is a massive failure. The UN cannot even agree on a definition for 'terrorism,' much less make it a crime. The UNRWA is a sinkhole, having spent billions on a massive infrastructure that still traps Palestinians in refugee camps after so many years. UNRWA should at least be funded by the Arab League, or better yet, folded into the UNHCR.

The UN has some agencies that undertake health, sanitation and development tasks. I expect these projects could function better by bi-lateral agreements between donor countries and recipients, rather than through the albatross of the UNGA and its glut of self-serving NGOs.

ISRAEL SHOULD NOT BE ALONE ON IRAN
Wall Street Journal, October 17, 2013

Israel will have to stop Iran, alone, if necessary, because it knows it is Iran's first target.

Regarding Yossi Klein Halevi's "A Lesson From the Yom Kippur War for a Perilous Time."

Prime Minister Golda Meir feared Richard Nixon and Henry Kissinger in 1973, and Israel paid a heavy price. Benjamin Netanyahu has no illusions about President Obama, but the stakes today are immense as compared with 40 years ago.

Israel will have to stop Iran because it knows it is Iran's first target. The leaders of Europe and America continue to procrastinate, hoping Iran will change its goals or that they will be able to manage the regime.

Europe cared little for the fate of Jews in the 1930s, and today hostility toward Jews and Israel is palpable, particularly in Britain, France, Norway and Sweden, where massive Muslim immigration is spreading instability.

Europe and the U.S. have as much to lose as does Israel, but they haven't got the fortitude to do anything about it. Just as they spoke of "peace in our time" while Hitler prepared for war, so are they now wishing away reality while the jihad is gathering steam. I suspect many in EU and U.S. governments are content to have Israel do their dirty work for them.

INSANE U-TURN!
Gulf Daily News, Bahrain, November 16, 2013

In the 1930s, British and American leaders watched impotently as Germany prepared to plunge the world into darkness. Today we are at an identical watershed; a raving dictatorship gearing up to dominate its region and become a major player on the world stage.

France remembers the swastika flying from the Arc De Triomphe.

President Obama has gone from "Iran will not get a nuclear weapon" to "America will not allow Iran to bomb Israel."

That is a huge policy shift. Obama is now prepared to allow Iran to continue enriching uranium, manufacture centrifuges and to build a plutonium reactor near Arak. The West will also drop sanctions and free up $50 billion in revenue. In return, Iran will promise not to use what it builds.

Do President Obama and Prime Minister Cameron really believe Iran will go to all this effort and not build a bomb? Have they forgotten their own people murdered by Iranian terrorism? Do they doubt Iran's resolve? Or, do they just want "peace in our time?"

Merci *mille fois*, President Hollande, for applying the brakes to this nefarious proposal.

IRAN DEAL
Miami Herald, December 3, 2013
U.S. puts Americans first.

Re: The Nov. 27 letter *Netanyahu shouldn't whine.*

Who threw whom "under the bus?" Jimmy Carter threw our ally, the shah of Iran, under the bus. President Obama threw allies Moammar Gadhafi and Hosni Mubarak out as well.

Yes, "Israel is totally capable of taking care of itself," but American interference undermined it during the Suez conflict and forced it to take the first hit in the Yom Kippur war. Israel is America's best friend, but the United States always does "what is right for Americans first."

LITTLE TOWN, BETHLEHEM
Irish Independent, December 28, 2013

Christmas, 2013, and excited tourists are milling around Bethlehem's Manger Square, stopping in restaurants and souvenir shops and enjoying the marching bands and scout troops performing next to the large tree in front of the Church of the Nativity.

Some 25,000 visitors are expected this year, up from recent years but way below the crowds that filled the area between 1967 and 2000.

In 1967, Christians made up 80pc of Bethlehem's population.

During the period from the Six-Day War to Arafat's intifada, there were no barriers to traffic between Israel, Gaza and the West Bank/Judea and Samaria. Muslims, Christians and Jews traveled back and forth to work, shop and play.

Everyone benefited.

The 1993-95 Oslo Accords marked the beginning of the end of Christian Bethlehem.

Bethlehem's Christians were forced out and the PLO confiscated their properties. As conditions worsened, more families, who had lived there for centuries, fled. Today, Bethlehem is predominantly Muslim.

In 2000, following the Camp David talks between Clinton, Arafat and Barak, Arafat began the second Intifada.

This ended the peaceful commerce the region had enjoyed and Bethlehem became more isolated. Even the Church of the Nativity was later over-run and desecrated by PLO fighters.

Israel built the security barrier to thwart terror attacks, and it has been relatively effective.

The passage through the barrier near Bethlehem is lightly guarded and traffic flows through, slowing but rarely stopping.

At this time of year, we can all hope for success in the Palestinian-Israeli peace talks.

Rebuttal: Bethlehem's Beauty

Referring to Saturday's letter on Bethlehem, yes it is beautiful—I spent nine days there a few years ago and really enjoyed the experience.

I visited the manger at 6:30am one morning and the atmosphere was magical but, later on in the day, it was ruined by the Israeli army corralling the Palestinians into pens as they got on to buses.

It was harrowing for them and they have to put up with it every time they wish to leave or re-enter their town. Surely the PLO are not responsible for that as Len Bennett seems to think? Anybody who has visited the area will be aware of the continuous harassment the Palestinians have to endure as a daily consequence of the Israeli land grab.

It is unfortunate that so many Christians have left the area but, perhaps if pilgrims stayed in the West Bank rather than Jerusalem, it would provide a livelihood for some Christians. —Gemma, *Westport*

2014

WORLD'S MORALITY IS IN QUESTION
Windsor Star, January 13, 2014

Re: Thousands of African migrants demand rights in protest outside Israel's parliament, by Tia Goldenberg.

Is there another country on the face of this Earth that has been more compassionate to immigrants than Israel?

Israel is a tiny country which has absorbed millions of refugees. I am not referring only to the Jews forced out of the Arab world or the Soviet Jews or the European Jews who "live in fear in Europe" according to the president of the European Parliament.

I am referring to the Christians, gays, Bedouin, Baha'i and others, including Africans, who fled persecution in African and Arab states.

Israel is the one shining light in the region but can it absorb everyone seeking a better life? Why are these refugees Israel's problem?

Where is the United Nations? Where are the huge, wealthy, oil nations? What are their responsibilities?

How dare the UN High Commission for Refugees lament Israel's incarceration of migrants, claiming it caused hardship and suffering and was not in line with a 1951 world treaty on the treatment of refugees?

This indictment from the organization that forced Palestinian Arabs to languish on welfare in refugee camps in Lebanon, Syria and areas under Fatah and Hamas control for 66 years. The UN's hypocrisy is shameless.

The African refugees are not in danger today. They made it out of their countries.

Now, the world community should work to provide them safe haven. It is the world's morality that is in question.

It is disingenuous and provocative to only target Israel.

MIDEAST PROCESS NOT PAINFUL
Miami Herald, January 12, 2014

What is Uri Dromi thinking in his Jan. 10 article, Time for Israel to reconsider Arab League peace offer? There is nothing "out of the box" about the 2002 Arab League "comprehensive peace initiative."

The Arab League proposal demanded a complete capitulation by Israel to return to the 1949 armistice lines and allow anyone, and their descendants, to move to Israel. In return, there would be a peace treaty with all Arab countries. Simply stated, Israel would be allowed to exist, however, up to 5 million new Muslim citizens and Jews would have no access to the new country of Palestine, including the Jewish Quarter of the old city of Jerusalem.

So Israel would be another Arab majority country, but Jews would be allowed to live there, unlike in the rest of the Arab world where they, as well as other "infidels," have been forced out. I have a hard time seeing the "painful process" the Arabs would be faced with.

SHARON: LOVE HIM OR HATE HIM
Toronto Star, January 19, 2014

Re: The greater national tragedy of Ariel Sharon.

Make no mistake about it. Ariel Sharon was a hero, defending his country in the 1950's against the combined strength of the Arab world, particularly Transjordan's Arab Legions, trained and supplied by Great Britain.

From 1950 to October 1953, armed marauders constantly infiltrated from the West Bank near Qibya, killing 89 and wounding 101, many victims being farmers and Holocaust survivors. Young Major Sharon was ordered to bombard the town and 69 people were killed. Following the attack, the Arab Legion forces deployed on the border near Qibya to stop further Arab infiltrations and Israeli reprisals.

Sabra and Shatila was an attack by Lebanese Christian Phalange militias against the Palestinians because the Palestinians bombed the parliament, killing the Christian president and members of his family and cabinet.

President Bashir Gemayel, who invited the Israelis to help route the PLO, signed a peace treaty with Israel, which was torn up upon his death.

No country except Israel would have held its generals to such a standard, claiming he should have made sure the opposing sides were kept apart. This would be like blaming Georges Bush for 9-11 because he didn't prevent it from happening. When Time Magazine accused Sharon with being responsible, they were sued and lost the libel trial.

As for the second intifada, Sharon had nothing to do with it. It was a plan hatched by Yasser Arafat even before he went to meet Ehud Barak and Bill Clinton at Camp David. Thousands of tourists visit the Temple Mount and Sharon was just one of them.

The result of Arafat unleashing suicide bombers on innocent civilians was the destruction of the cooperation between Israelis and Palestinians. The Israeli economy was badly hurt and the Palestinian economy was destroyed. The separation barrier was necessary to reduce terrorism and it works. This so fractured Palestinian society that now Fatah and Hamas are engaged in a virtual civil war.

Many will always blame Israel for everything that goes wrong for the Palestinians. How could Sharon or any Israeli be a hero?

No Pandering
Calgary Herald, January 25, 2014

Re: Hidden agenda on jaunt to Israel.

Rob Keith has no valid reason for suspecting the inclusion of Shawn Ketcheson in the prime minister's Middle East visit. I would think someone who possesses the moral leadership to speak his truth and who promotes a values-based foreign policy would be an asset.

It is a point of pride that Canada has its own position on foreign policy. Canada, like Israel, is a liberal democratic society, where divergent views are respected.

As for the makeup of the delegation, what political motives can the PM have? With 315,000 Jews and 1,050,000 Muslims in Canada, I do not see any racial or religious pandering objective in this visit.

UN Must Take A Stand
Canadian Jewish News, January 30, 2014

Surely this is the last straw ("UNESCO exhibit cancellation slammed.") Can any civilized person not recognize the overt and shameless anti-Semitism displayed by the Arab League and the United Nations? Hitler and Goebbels would be proud of them. If the leaders of the democracies don't immediately demand an apology from the UN and a restoration of the program, then the clash of civilizations is lost, and the jihadists have won. The exhibition, The People, the Book, the Land – 3,500 years of ties between the Jewish People and the Land of Israel, deserves to be seen on UN property. No group of racists should be allowed to dominate the UN and subvert it from its mission, part of which is "to practice tolerance and live together in peace with one another as good neighbors."

For The Record
Gulf Daily News, Bahrain, March 22, 2014

This refers to "A new world disorder". This article ignores much of the refugee issues created when the UN decided to divide Palestine into a Jewish state and an Arab state.

The UN listed 710,000 Palestinian Arab refugees. A refugee was anyone who had lived in what is now Israel for two years. The UNRWA, a separate agency that handles only Palestinian Arabs, considers all descendants of the original Arab refugees to also be refugees, a classification never given to any other people.

There were also 10,000 Jewish Palestinian refugees from Gaza and the West Bank, as well as 870,000 forced out of Mena (Middle East and North Africa.)

600,000 found a haven in Israel. The Arabs placed many of their brethren into refugee camps in Gaza, the West Bank. Lebanon, Syria and Jordan.

There is still an Arab Palestinian problem for three reasons. The UN will not close UNRWA and turn the issue over to UNHCR, the agency tasked to resolve all refugee issues. There is animus between local populations and the Palestinians, partly due to the civil wars they started in Jordan and Lebanon and their support of Iraq when it invaded Kuwait. And, finally, the Arab League wants it that way.

As for the assertion that settlements are the problem, there were no settlements in 1967 when Arab armies launched their third war against Israel.

Rebuttal: A brutal occupation

This is in response to the letter "For the record." There are some Arab Palestinian Israelis, but they represent a small minority of Palestinians, and they do not have equal rights to Jewish citizens.

With regards to the statistics of the original Palestinian Arab refugees, today's numbers do not reflect merely those refugees and their descendants.

Israel has continually created new refugees since its inception, through various means and tactics. Chaim Weizmann, founder and first president of Israel, while publicly reassuring Palestinians, wrote in his autobiography that ultimately it was his desire for Palestine to become "as Jewish as England is English".

The ethnic and religious distribution of Palestine had been well documented before the creation of the state of Israel. How do you turn an Arab country, with a very small Jewish minority, into a Jewish state, if you don't get rid of the non-Jewish residents?

It has been a long, slow, chronic process, but it is still ethnic cleansing.

Zionism, by definition is a racist, colonial ideology (the movement to establish and further a Jewish State in Palestine - Webster's Encyclopedia of Dictionaries ,1981). In Ben Gurion's private diary, July 18, 1948, it is said: "We must do everything to ensure they do not return."

Many of Israel's great leaders also discussed in their private writings, methods for disinheriting the indigenous population, (Theodore Herzl's Tagebuches, Vol. II, p.24 1898). Others commented on "the problem" of settling a land that was already settled (Sheean Vincent, 1935).

Others created or spread propaganda for public consumption. Everyone has heard, for example, the phrase, "The land without people, for people without land" (Zangwill, 1901), and Golda Meir reiterated not allowing any Palestinians to return and also stated, "There was no such thing as Palestinians.

It was not as though there was a Palestinian people considering itself a Palestinian people and we came and threw them out and took their country away from them. They did not exist" (Quoted in The Sunday Times, June 15, 1969).

In 1968, UNRWA Commissioner-General John H Davis wrote in "The Evasive Peace", (page 57) "the extent to which the refugees were savagely driven out by the Israelis as part of a deliberate master-plan has been sufficiently recognized."

The list goes on and on and on.

The problem with past peace deals is that they did not acknowledge, or they compromised the rights of the refugees either to return or for compensation.

Settlements are land grabs. Negotiations are a distraction. Every time they return to negotiations, they step up the building of settlements on Palestinian land. Where else in the civilized world are stateless people still subjected to colonial occupation? How is it a democracy if so many people don't count? If they cannot allow Palestinians a viable land of their own, give them real equal rights and let go of the idea of being a "Jewish" state. —*Lisa*

'Glick Plan' Problems
Jerusalem Post, March 28, 2014

The 'Glick plan' ("A bold proposal," Books, review of Caroline Glick's *The Israeli Solution*) is interesting, but [the plan] contains three glaring errors.

First; it assumes the Arab world would tolerate an infidel country in its midst. The PLO occupied much of Lebanon in the 1970s and '80s. They started a civil war which saw 700,000 Lebanese Christians flee the country, ending the rule of the only Christian Middle East entity. The PLO/PA, Hamas and the Arab League will never agree to hand the reins of power to Israel.

Second; the Arabs claim there are now five million Palestinian Arab refugees. One reason the current round of peace talks are floundering is because [PA head Mahmoud] Abbas insists these refugees have a "right" to move into pre-1967 Israel. Could Israel possibly survive if the refugee camps in Gaza, the West Bank, Lebanon, Syria and Jordan, plus everyone else who claims a relationship to Mandatory Palestine were to flood into Israel? The U.N. definition of a refugee is anyone who spent two years in Palestine and all their descendants. We see how Muslims have staked out chunks of Europe, have driven the infidels from their no-go zones and are driving out the Jews. The same would happen in Israel.

And third; assuming the Arab League thought this was a good idea, how could Israel possibly support millions of Arabs, bred on hatred for Jews and educated on revenge and terrorism? The world of Islam is tribal. The turmoil in much of MENA shows exactly what would transpire. While Israeli Arabs live better than their brothers, with proportional representation in civil society and the military, an influx of millions would overwhelm Israel economically and socially. An Arab majority would be inevitable and Israel would replicate the Lebanese experience.

SOME CAN FLEE TO ISRAEL TO ESCAPE PERSECUTION
Windsor Star, April 4, 2014

Re: Group in for long haul, by Paul Chislett.

Another Canadian school has fallen victim to the pernicious racism that is anti-Semitism.

What possible logic could these pseudo-intellectuals rely on to castigate the only liberal democracy in the Middle East? Are they so swayed by the Muslim brotherhood funded Arab students' clubs?

Israel is the one haven in the Mideast where gays, Christians, Baha'i, Bedouin and Africans can flee to escape persecution throughout the Arab world.

Israeli Arabs are the only free Arabs in the region. They vote, they have political parties and members in the Knesset and enjoy the finest universities and hospitals in the world.

There is an Arab on Israel's Supreme Court. Arabs represent 20 per cent of the Israeli Defense Forces, including the officers' ranks.

Israel's neighbors hang gays, murder infidels, burn churches, consider their woman as chattel, keep slaves and have confined Palestinian-Arab refugees on UN welfare in camps in Gaza, the West Bank, Lebanon, Syria and Jordan for generations.

U of W's Jew haters reject Canadian values. They should throw away their computers, iPhones and iPads that are making Israel rich.

ARAB LEAGUE'S 'NO' REFRAIN
Jerusalem Post, April 25, 2014

Once again, the Arab League has destroyed the possibility of a Palestinian state.

Once again, the Arab League has forced an impotent Palestinian leadership to reject peace with Israel and a state of Palestine.

Once again, the Arab League is condemning thousands of Palestinian Arab refugees to languish in camps in Gaza, the West Bank, Lebanon, Syria and Jordan.

On March 25, 2014, the League promised no recognition of Israel as a Jewish state, no concession on the 'right of return' of Arab refugees to Israel and no end-of-conflict resolution. This was a restatement of the 1967 Khartoum Declaration which proclaimed no peace with Israel, no negotiations with Israel and no recognition of Israel. It also echoed Arafat's rejection of the Clinton Camp David talks in 2000 when Arafat too would not agree to end the conflict. Arafat clearly insisted the next generation had the right to determine whether they wished to try once again to destroy Israel.

In defiance of UNSC Resolution 242 and U.S. foreign policy, Abbas has applied to join 18 UN agencies. The non-existent state of Palestine will certainly be admitted to all of them. The United Nations is dominated and controlled by the 57-member block of Muslim countries, though it is financed largely by the American taxpayer.

The Americans and Secretary Kerry have wasted a lot of energy and political capital on the dream of 2 states for 2 peoples. It was futile in light of Islamic rejection of any infidel presence in the Middle East. As Christian Lebanon was destroyed, so too must Jewish Israel. In light of

Arab rejection, the US must now take concrete steps. This administration must turn away from the Muslim Brotherhood advisors they've relied on and cut funding to the Palestinian Authority and any UN agencies that recognize Palestine as a state.

CUT OPEC UMBILICAL CORD
Miami Herald, April 29, 2014

The key point of the Keystone XL pipeline debate should be whether the United States or Saudi Arabia will control our economy and national policies.

So long as we are not in control of our energy, we will be manipulated by the OPEC potentates. They decide what Americans will pay at the gas pump and for our heating fuel as we continue to transfer funds from our coffers to theirs. When our economy is on the rise, they can bleed off any benefit we should be enjoying.

While this administration considers the Muslim Brotherhood to be moderate and has highly placed associates in positions of power and influence, the Brotherhood still is the headquarters of Sunni terrorism world-wide and its interests are not ours.

A major step toward reclaiming our values should be to partner with Canada for continental energy independence and to cut the OPEC umbilical cord. The nicety of cleaner energy can be explored once we are in control of our energy, our internal and foreign policies and our wallets.

KERRY 'RETARDED THE PEACE PROCESS'
National Post, April 30, 2014

Re: Kerry Breaks 'Apartheid' Taboo.

By becoming the first American official to the use the word "apartheid" in relation to Israel, U.S. Secretary of State John Kerry has joined the ranks of the anti-Semites. Israel is the only country in the Middle East that does not practice apartheid. Ask the 850,000 Jews forced out of their homes in the Middle East and North Africa. Ask the 700,000 Christian Lebanese forced out during the PLO occupation of their country. Ask Bethlehem's Christians, 80% of whom were forced out by the PLO. Ask the women and gays of the Arab world. Ask the Coptic Christians of Egypt, or the Bedouin who fled into Israel from Gaza. Mr. Kerry has disgraced himself and retarded the peace process. President Barack Obama should fire him and Israel should place him on its no-fly list.

POPE'S MIDDLE EAST TRIP
Wall Street Journal, June 4, 2014

Re: Pope's Middle East Trip Highlights Plight of Christians.

Pope Francis took a dramatic plunge into Arab-Israeli politics last week. He and the Israelis both support a sovereign Palestinian state living in peace and security alongside the Jewish state.

Unfortunately, the pope was manipulated by his Arab hosts on his visit to the disputed territories. The stop at the separation barrier was blatantly staged for maximum propaganda value. That wasn't a random section of the barrier. This was a newly painted section of carefully applied, anti-Semitic, pseudo graffiti.

The Pope missed the opportunity of asking the Palestinian Authority, the Arab League and the United Nations Relief and Works Agency for Palestine Refugees why there are still refugee camps, all under Arab control, 66 years after five Arab armies and local militias attacked the newborn State of Israel. He should have asked why they haven't been integrated into the vast lands of the 27 Arab states.

A prayer meeting is very nice, but the participants must realize that until the Arab League accepts the 1947 UN resolution creating an Arab and a "Jewish" state, nothing Israel does will end the conflict.

Details Of Palestinian Experience
In Lebanon Lacking
Windsor Star, July 3, 2014

Re: He's got the power at refugee camp, by Ryan Lucas.

In his human interest story about a Palestinian electrician, Ryan Lucas, from The Associated Press, gives a brief but very incomplete and misleading background to the history of the Palestinian experience in Lebanon.

There were two migrations of Palestinian Arabs into Lebanon. The first was a consequence of the 1948 Arab-Israeli war. The second, known as Black September, was in 1972, when the PLO was forced out of Jordan following their attempt to overthrow the Hashemite kingdom.

The PLO then occupied southern Lebanon. They terrorized and taxed the people and were instrumental in the civil war which forced 700,000 Christians out of the country. They also used Lebanon as a base for attacks against Israel.

On June 6, 1982, Israel entered Lebanon to rout out the PLO. They signed a peace treaty with newly elected president Bashir Gemayel. On Sept. 14, 1982, because of his pact with Israel, the president and 26 members of his Christian Phalange Kataeb party were murdered at their Beirut headquarters.

Two days later, in retaliation, Phalange militiamen snuck into Sabra and Shatila and massacred hundreds of Palestinian and Lebanese Shiites.

The PLO was forced to flee to Tunis and the remaining Palestinians were never accepted into Lebanese society.

Readers React To Arrests For The Murder Of The Israeli-Arab Teen, Muhammad Khdeir
Jerusalem Post, July 11, 2014

The Hamas terrorists have opened the 'gates of hell' and now they will see what's on the other side.

How dare President Barack Obama urge "all parties to refrain from steps that could further destabilize the situation?"

How dare UN secretary general Ban Ki-moon urge "all parties to refrain from any actions that could further escalate this highly tense situation?"

How dare they make a moral equivalency between the terrorists who murdered three innocent teenagers on their way home from school and the state which is obligated to keep its people safe?

Obama should have offered his "deepest and heartfelt condolences" to the families and to the State of Israel and he should have cut off all funding to Hamas/Fatah.

Ban should have "issued a similar condemnation" and cut off all further UN funding to the terrorists and the areas they control.

In truth, the haste with which both Obama and Ki-moon welcomed the integration of Fatah and Hamas may have emboldened the terrorists' feeling they were invincible. They know they will always be treated gently by this American administration and the corrupt United Nations.

QUESTIONS OVER BBC's COVERAGE
OF ISRAEL-PALESTINE CRISIS
The Guardian, July 12, 2014

Hamas must be disarmed for the sake of both Israel and the Palestinian Authority. Hamas is recognized by the EU as a terrorist organization. Its charter calls for the destruction of Israel and it has fired thousands of rockets into civilian areas. Though no one has been killed recently, Hamas's goal with each shot was attempted mass murder. Hamas cannot be a partner with Fatah either. Can one imagine a government with its own army and 10,000 rockets? How can the central government in Ramallah exercise any control over this rogue entity? Only when Hamas is disarmed can there be a Palestinian government. Only then will the Palestinian authority have a chance of reaching a deal for a two-state solution. This depends, of course, on the Arab League deciding Israel has a right to exist in the Middle East. In the meantime, Hamas will use civilians as human shields, and women and children will die. Dead civilians (real or fake) will be a PR coup for the terrorists and anti-Semites worldwide will rant and rave.

ISRAEL WILL CONTINUE TO DEFEND ITSELF
Montreal Gazette, July 17, 2014

Re: Israel's lack of restraint in Gaza hurts prospects for peace.

Ayman Oweida is entitled to his opinions and they are welcome, however opinions should not be stated as facts.

Israel's so-called occupation is not illegal, any more than was the allied occupation of Germany after the Second World War, and the territories are disputed, not Palestinian, nor occupied. UN Security Council resolutions state the solution to the Israeli-Palestinian conflict will be decided by direct negotiations between the parties.

Israel is not deliberately bombing civilians. The use of private homes, public buildings and civilian hostages as implements of war by Hamas is a war crime.

The humanitarian crisis in Gaza is of Hamas's doing. They are in charge, not Israel.

Throughout the current fighting, Israel has supplied Gaza with electricity, food and supplies and has taken wounded Gaza residents to Israeli hospitals for treatment.

Nothing Israel does will anger or mollify those trained to hate Jews by their leaders, schools, mosques and media. In 1948, 1967 and 1973, Israel fought enemies whose clearly stated goal was genocide. Israel will continue to defend itself against those who reject its right to exist.

ISRAEL'S GOALS ARE HONORABLE
Sun-Sentinel, July 18, 2014

Israel does not want to maintain military control of another people, nor does it wish to be destroyed. The goal of Hamas, as well as Fatah and the Arab League, is the elimination of Israel. They have pledged repeatedly not to recognize Israel as a Jewish state (the UN did so in 1947) and to insist on allowing millions of Arabs into Israel.

They also refuse to consider an end-of-conflict resolution. What the Arabs want is to get as much as they can, with the help of the most anti-Israel American administration in history, without agreeing to a permanent peace treaty.

Hamas has been firing rockets into Israel for years. The organization started this round of hostilities, with the murders of the three teenagers, in an attempt to develop credibility within the Islamist community. Just as al-Qaeda became prominent on 9/11, Hamas is attempting to break out of the rut in which it finds itself.

Hamas is bankrupt. When the Muslim Brotherhood was thrown out of Egypt, it lost its easy access to goods, materials and weapons smuggled in from Sinai. Even though Hamas and Fatah have signed an agreement, Fatah won't pay Gaza's public servants, who have not had any salaries in over a year. Fatah even refused to allow funding from Qatar to be passed through to Hamas.

Hamas and Hezbollah are fighting each other in Syria, so another support link has been severed. Hamas' only steadfast ally is Iran, the source of its weaponry.

If Hamas can score a major hit in Tel Aviv or Jerusalem, it will become important again and funding will start pouring in from Islamic charities around the world. It is Israel's job to make sure Hamas fails. Israel must disarm Hamas. The EU and UN must not give Hamas another chance to terrorize Israelis and Palestinian Arabs.

CONFLICT IS ABOUT SURVIVAL
Calgary Herald, July 30, 2014

Re: Unite the Middle East.

Does Anwar Sultan not remember that when the United Nations partitioned Palestine into a Jewish state and an Arab state in 1947, Israel chose peace while the Arabs chose a war to drive the Jews into the sea? That is the core of the Arab-Israeli conflict and it continues unabated today.

It is not settlements in Judea and Samaria.

It's Tel Aviv. It's not Israel's security barrier or the Gaza blockade. It's Israel's right to defend itself and its people against annihilation.

The Arabs, led by Haj Amin al-Husseini, the Grand Mufti of Jerusalem, were allied with Hitler in the Second World War. Hamas and its supporters are still fighting that war.

Hamas is a terrorist organization. Fatah, while it supports terrorism from time to time, has a chance of creating a Palestinian state, living in peace alongside Israel.

All it needs is the Arab League's support, which to date has refused to accept infidel Israel in its midst.

Hamas must be disarmed for the sake of both Israel and the Palestinians. The U.S. and the EU must not rescue Hamas again, nor should they continue funding them.

INVESTIGATE THE UN
Calgary Herald, August 28, 2014

If only the United Nations would hold both Israelis and Palestinians to account. However, they never have and they won't during this sham inquiry.

The UN, dominated by the 57-member bloc of the Organization of Islamic Cooperation, is blatantly anti-Semitic. The UN Human Rights Council is its most cynical tentacle, whose membership includes China, Kuwait, Saudi Arabia, Algeria, Pakistan, Russia and the United Arab Emirates. Not one of these countries even feigns respect for a free press, a separate judiciary or minorities, women and gays.

UN Human Rights Commissioner Navi Pillay has not a word to say about the persecution of Baha'is, Yazidis or Christians, but Israel defending itself against internationally recognized terrorists got her attention.

It is the UN, the UNHRC and UN Relief and Works Agency who should be investigated by an independent commission. It is they who have engaged in the collective punishment of the Arab refugees from the 1948 war to push the Jews into the sea.

It is they who keep them trapped in Arab-controlled refugee camps while their leaders grow rich.

It is they, with Hamas, who should be held accountable for the Gaza war and the decades-old war of military and political attrition against Israel. An impartial investigation should be held, led by a group of democracies, far away from the UN.

READERS CONTINUE TO WRITE IN ON
OPERATION PROTECTIVE EDGE
Jerusalem Post, August 22, 2014

Israel stands alone. Anti-Semitism is the standard and common denominator of both left and right-wing ideologues. World leaders either support, or are afraid of the terrorists. Reporters of the so-called free press are the useful idiots of every fascist dictator they want to interview.

Why would anyone support another truce between Palestinian terrorists and the free, democratic state of Israel? What is needed is an end to the Arab-Israeli conflict, which is the product of Arab rejection of the United Nations' 1947 resolution to split what was left of the British Mandate for Palestine into Jewish and Arab states.

Arabs attacked Israel in three wars of genocide; 1948, 1967 and 1973. Where are the UN condemnations? Where are the boycott movements against them? Where are the war crimes charges?

When UN Resolution 181 was passed, there were 58 member countries and most of them were relatively free. Today there are 193 member states. Most are dictatorships or sham-democracies. Few are truly free, have independent judiciaries, an open press or respect the rights of minorities, women and gays. The UN is ground zero in the war against the Jews, dominated by the 57-member Organization of Islamic Cooperation.

The Gaza blockade is not the main stumbling block to the Cairo truce plan. The main obstacle is the rejection of Israel's right to exist. Once the OIC accepts that the only free county in the Middle East has a right to be there, peace will follow.

As for the EU or the UN patrolling Gaza, the experience in Lebanon should suffice to ridicule that notion. Under UN-supervision, Hezbollah imported 60,000 rockets, despite UNSC Resolution 1701, which was meant to disarm them. The UN became Hezbollah's protectors.

The current Hamas-Israel war must lead to an end of the conflict, not another truce.

Enemy Must Be Named
Calgary Herald, September 3, 2014

Re: RCMP takes issue with 'adversarial' tone of Muslim handbook.

Kudos to the RCMP for seeing through the deception the Islamic Social Services Association and the National Council of Canadian Muslims tried to foist on the Canadian law enforcement community. This is an example of stealth jihadism under the noble cover of United Against Terrorism, a program, purportedly meant to dissuade Muslim youth from becoming radicalized but would do little more than clothe Islamic terrorism in terms that ignore its core components.

Ever since 14-year-old Aisha watched, with her husband Mohammad, the beheading of 800 Jewish men and prepubescent boys of the Qurayza tribe in 627 AD, and their women and infants taken as slaves, violence has been part of Islamic expansion.

To deny the millions of "infidel" deaths over the centuries due to Islamist supremacist ideology is to deny truth. To forbid the use of words to describe these acts is calumny.

Radical Islam is radical Islam. Jihad, to many Muslims, is the moral duty to convert or slay the non-believer.

It is not the use of terminology by Canadian authorities that is radicalizing young Muslims. It is what they learn at their mosques, 80 per cent of which were Saudi funded and imbued with Wahhabism, a radical form of Islam. If we cannot name the enemy, we cannot defeat it.

Is Israel Justified In Building New Settlements?
National Post, September 4, 2014

When discussing the proposed Israeli settlement, we need to get our facts straight. Firstly, it's a housing project in Judea and Samaria, not a settlement in the West Bank. Second, it is not Palestinian land. There is no such thing until there is a Palestinian state. There is no Palestine because the Arab League doesn't want one. All the Arabs wants is to rid the neighborhood of the infidel state of Israel. The Palestinian Arabs, both Hamas and Fatah, have no independent capacity to act, nor do they want to live in peace alongside the Jewish state.

If they wanted a new Arab state next to Israel, they could have had it in 1948, 1967, 1973 and under the Clinton/Rabin and Olmert plans, but they didn't want it. They are accustomed to the role of UN welfare bums.

So stop gnashing your teeth over the poor Palestinians. If they wanted a country, they'd sign a peace treaty with Israel and set up an internationally recognized border within which they could build as they wished, and so could the Israelis on their side of the border. But the Arabs would have to forgo the dream of destroying Israel and that's not what they want.

By the way, this new plot of land Israel is planning to build on was considered by the Bush administration as an area Israel would keep in any eventual peace deal. U.S. President Barack Obama and the Palestinian Authority know this.

UN Is Guilty Of War Crimes
Canadian Jewish News, September 11, 2014

The United Nations has let loose William Schabas, supported by UN Human Rights Commissioner Navi Pillay, to lecture and threaten Israel and to produce a report whose prejudicial conclusions will paint Israel in a bad light ("UNHRC commission chair dismisses allegation of bias."

Schabas and Pillay are part of an ignoble group of human rights violators that includes Algeria, China, Cuba, Kuwait, Pakistan, Russia, Saudi Arabia and the United Arab Emirates. It is the UN, with its many anti-Semitic bodies that are guilty of war crimes, not Israel.

The UNHRC feigns concern about the deaths of Palestinians, but not Israelis, Baha'is, Yazidis, Christians, gays or women. Israel tells civilians where to go to remain safe, while Hamas has killed people trying to leave and forced others to remain in the combat zones.

It is Hamas who is committing crimes against humanity and must be held accountable but, at the UN, racism and petro-dollars trump truth

CRITICISM TOLERATED
Miami Herald, September 17, 2014

Re: Elite Israeli spies refuse to target Palestinians.

This is a telling story. Forty-three soldiers protesting what they regard as injustices, and they are able to speak to the media without fear. What a gloriously open society Israel is to accept such criticism as part of the give-and-take of democracy, even while the country is on a war-footing.

It is interesting too that 20 percent of Israel's military, including the officers' corps, is Arab, and every one of them is a volunteer. Also, 20 percent of students in Israeli universities are Arab as well, in exact proportion to their percentage of the population.

I wonder how any Islamic entity would respond to similar protests from its fighters?

A TRAGEDY AT THE OPERA
New York Post, September 24, 2014

How can the city victimized by 9/11 present an opera glorifying terrorism ("Met Opera's Uncivil 'Art,' " Judea Pearl, Post Opinion, Sept. 23)?

"The Death of Klinghoffer" has no right to the fabled stage of the Metropolitan Opera. This work glorifies the Palestine Liberation Organization's hijacking of a cruise ship and the shameful murder of an old man in a wheelchair.

What should have been a study of the mentality and cowardice of Islamofascism was turned into a vehicle to excuse the terrorists' actions. This anti-Semitic opera is a disgrace and will be viewed as a propaganda victory for the forces determined to destroy the freedoms we in the West cherish. This is a stain on the reputations of the Met, its audience and its sponsors.

CANADA'S ROLE IN WAR AGAINST ISLAMIC STATE
Toronto Star, September 27, 2014

Re: Obama scores coalition victory with Syria airstrikes.

President Obama is proud to stand shoulder to shoulder with Saudi Arabia (which funded 9/11), the United Arab Emirates, Jordan, Bahrain and Qatar. With the exception of Jordan, none are our friends.

None are countries in the traditional understanding of the term. They are all family-owned businesses. None of the royals has a modicum of interest in human rights. They relish beheadings for non-violent offenses. Women are commodities to be sexually exploited for the enjoyment of the powerful. Gays and minorities lead a tenuous existence.

The royal families live lavishly off the oil wealth they neither discovered nor developed. These tribal kings have contributed nothing to the world. Now, as IS/ISIS/ISIL is running rampant over Iraq and Syria, they know they are in the cross-hairs of the jihadist terrorists they have so often supported.

We now have the U.S. fighting to save the Islamic kings who have fleeced us for decades, polluting our governments and universities and undermining our democracy. The goal of these new-found allies is still the same as that of the Muslim Brotherhood, Al Qaeda, Hamas, ISIS, etc. They all work towards our demise and the establishment of a caliphate.

Is Obama the champ, or the chump, of the Middle East?

PROSPECT OF A NEW INTIFADA IN PALESTINIAN TERRITORIES
The Guardian, October 3, 2014

Israel's long term objective is a two-state solution, with Israelis and Palestinians living side by side in peace and security. Arabs should remember the good old days, from 1967 to Arafat's intifada, when there were no restrictions on Jewish and Arab movement from the river to the sea. Everyone traveled back and forth to work, shop and play. Gaza's beaches were a favorite vacation spot for young Israelis.

Peace with Israel would allow Palestinians to share in the dynamism of Israeli creativity and commerce. Destroying Israel would not be in their best interest. Neighboring states would quickly swallow them up. Palestinians must decide if ideology is more important than a rich and modern life for their families.

The British And Swedish Message
Jerusalem Post, October 31, 2014

Did the British parliament send a message to Israel or to the free world?

The UK, like Sweden, voted to recognize a Palestinian state. Half the British parliamentarians didn't have the backbone to vote, so the vote was carried by a minority of members. But, what is Palestine?

Palestine is the invention of Yasser Arafat, an Egyptian, who forced his idea onto the world stage by using terrorism to focus our attention. His concept was to remove the infidels from Israel and to replace them with the Arab refugees who fled or were forced out of the area following the UN Partition Plan of 1947, as well as all their descendants. The inclusion of the children and grandchildren of refugees was a new and exclusive idea, allowed only for Palestinian Arabs, and is aided and abetted by UNRWA, a gargantuan, corrupt agency which has kept the refugees in horrid camps for decades.

Palestine has no visible means of support. It has no borders nor capacity to govern. It exists solely on welfare. Its components have always relied on terrorism as a bargaining tool.

Britain, like Sweden, Norway, France and other areas of Europe (some say Eurabia) has been inundated with Islamic immigration which has overturned its society. Like London's Sharia enclave of Tower Hamlets, and Rotherham's child prostitution scandal, police and government agencies are loath to take on the Muslim mobs. One twitter post and thousands of Muslims take to the streets, as was demonstrated throughout Europe this summer when Israel dared to protect its civilians against Hamas rockets.

Europe is pretty much lost. It will continue to buckle under the demands of its hostile immigrants. Its policies will more and more reflect those of MENA (Middle East and North Africa) and it will ape the Council for Islamic Cooperation that dominates the UN.

Britain and Sweden are sending us a message. Beware of the Islamic Trojan horse.

HUMANIST PERSPECTIVES
Humanist Perspectives, October 18, 2014

This is an excellent article. It contains much valuable information on the history of Islam and its spread.

Permit me to point out some inaccuracies in the opening paragraphs.

In all modern warfare, the expected ratio of civilian to military deaths is between 3 to 1 and 5 to 1. The one glaring difference is Israel. In the recent Hamas-Israel conflict, the ratio was 1 to 1. The false UN numbers are directly from Hamas. In the previous Hamas-Israel conflict, the UN was forced to ultimately accept their numbers were wrong.

Israel knows everyone's addresses, their phone numbers and their cell numbers. This is how they warn civilians of upcoming attacks. They are also monitoring all calls (like CSIS or the CIA) and know the details of anyone killed from the calls and messages made. Even Mahmoud Abbas taunted Hamas that 850 Fatah fighters were killed, while only 80 Hamas members died in the latest Gaza fight.

Now, back to the modern rebirth of the Jewish homeland.

Modern Zionism started in the 1880's with Jewish immigration to what was a desolate part of the Ottoman Empire. As the Jews built farms and cities, Arabs from surrounding regions followed, seeking economic opportunities.

The British Mandate for Palestine was created by the victors of WWI and was the first time any place was called Palestine. The Brits quickly severed 80% of the mandate, creating Transjordan.

Prior to 1948, the only people who called themselves "Palestinians" were the Jews. The Arabs were Arabs or Egyptians or Syrians. The Palestine Post, the Jewish residents' newspaper, became the Jerusalem Post, which still publishes. The deserts and malarial swamps the Jews turned green was purchased from the major Arab families, including the

Husseinis, at inflated prices. No land was taken by violence.

In 1947, when the Arabs rejected the UN Partition Plan, 50% of the Arabs of Palestine were recent immigrants. The UN defines an Arab (not Palestinian) refugee as anyone who lost his home after living in Palestine for 2 or more years.

Life for Jews in the Arab world became intolerable. 850,000 Jews were forced penniless from their homes, most of them finding refuge in Israel. Within a few years, 50% of Israel's Jews were refugees from Arab lands.

You rightly point out the Islamists will never tolerate a Jewish state. Just as the PLO occupation of Lebanon drove out 700,000 Christians, Hamas/Fatah hopes to do the same to Israel.

Stop Insulting America's Only Ally In Mideast
Sun-Sentinel, November 4, 2014

How horrible of President Obama and Secretary Kerry to further damage the relationship between the U.S. and Israel.

The status quo between Israel and the Palestinians is unsustainable, as Kerry said, and the status quo between this administration and Israel is also unsustainable.

The American people and Congress support Israel. Israel is the only friend we have in the Middle East, the only nation that promotes our values and the only nation that wouldn't stab us in the back for a barrel of light sweet crude.

The Obama Administration is solidly in the Arab camp on the Arab-Israeli conflict.

The source of these well-planned remarks may be anonymous to The Atlantic, but they are not to the administration. If this leak does not reflect the president, then find the perpetrators and fire them. Anything less is disgraceful and unacceptable and damaging to America's image.

JIHAD IN JERUSALEM HAS NOTHING TO DO WITH STATEHOOD
Wall Street Journal, November 26, 2014

Once again we see the horror of Palestinian terrorism. Once again we see the result of Arab lies and incitement to violence by all Palestinian leaders.

When Jordan captured part of the Palestinian Mandate in 1948, they forced out every Jew, filled their homes with Arab settlers and destroyed dozens of Synagogues. One of the most prominent, the Hurva Synagogue, was re-opened this year.

In contrast, when Israel drove out Jordan in 1967, every religious property was respected and control was handed to the respective authorities. The Temple Mount was given to the Waqf. Every Israeli government since has reaffirmed that Jordan and the Jerusalem Islamic Waqf were in charge. It is they who decide who visits the Dome of the Rock and no infidel ever enters the Al-Aqsa Mosque.

Politically incorrect, or not, that's the core difference between Arabs and Jews.

The Arab League will not accept any infidel entity in control in the Middle East. The PLO drove the Christians from Lebanon. The PA did the same in Bethlehem. The Muslim Brotherhood destroyed churches and slaughtered Christians in Egypt during their short reign of terror. ISIS continues the work.

So long as Arabs celebrate murder with candies and cake and Western media gives them a pass, no matter how heinous the crime, and American and European leaders continue to pander to OPEC's owners, Islamists will enjoy the fruits of racism and terrorism and plan the coming Caliphate.

2015

Palestinian Authority's Move Legally Risk
Sun-Sentinel, January 6, 2015

Palestinian Authority President Mahmoud Abbas is being badly advised. If the PA becomes a member of the International Criminal Court and Israel does not, it is Israel who will have the upper hand. The PA could charge individuals with crimes, but have no way of bringing them to trial, unless they are captured in a member state.

On the other side, anyone who has suffered from Palestinian terrorism, be it rockets fired from Gaza or suicide bombings or other acts inspired by speeches or media, could charge the PA itself. The PA would have to answer the charges and, if found guilty would be liable for damages or incarceration.

The difference is that Israel would not have to present anyone to the court, but the PA would have to send charged people to The Hague. So members of Abbas's government, leaders of Hamas, Islamic Jihad or other military groups, heads of TV stations and imams could, and likely will, be charged by individuals or groups for incitement to violence and for crimes against humanity. They will have to defend themselves or be found guilty. If the court rules against the PA, its funds anywhere in the world could be seized.

The PA and the Arab League can get what they want through the U.N. General Assembly, where resolutions are not legally binding. Inviting the ICC to probe the PA and its people, with lawyers presenting evidence on both sides is a different story.

READERS REACT TO LAST WEEK'S PARIS BLOODSHED
Jerusalem Post, January 16, 2015

Most commentators miss the big picture. Charlie Hebdo was just the rational for this attack on our freedoms by radical Muslims, intent on destroying our way of life and replacing it with a Caliphate.

Whether it's a cartoon, a Jewish supermarket, men at prayer, a video, a Coptic church, little girls in Rotherham, people waiting for a tram or running a marathon, there will always be a reason for Islamic terrorists to resort to violence and murder. There will always be something that offends the Islamists. A woman's visible hair defines her as a prostitute. Singing children are evil. Infidels are an insult to the true believer.

The target is incidental to the act. Just as Islam means "submission," the focus of radical Islam is the sublimation of the rest of society to Islam.

Obviously, most Muslims would not resort to violence, but all studies show the vast majority support and cheer the Islamists. Western nations, liberal by nature, will ignore this reality at their peril.

We must recognize there is a straight line from the Muslim Brotherhood, with its ties to the Obama administration, to CAIR (Council on American-Islamic Relations), MSA (Muslim Students Association), Hamas, ISIS etc. The internecine conflict between Sunnis and Shi'ites is subordinate to the fight against the infidel and our freedom and independence.

Much of Europe, particularly France, Britain, Norway and Sweden have been strangled by massive Islamic immigration. This should be a warning to others.

BAIRD MET WITH HURLED EGGS, SHOES IN RAMALLAH
Ottawa Citizen, January 29, 2015

What a disgrace. How dare these protesters, behaving like punks, throw eggs at Canadian Foreign Affairs Minister John Baird? And, how dare the chief Palestinian negotiator Saeb Erekat chastise Canada for it?

Canada supports an Independent Palestinian state living in peace and security alongside Israel. It seems the Palestinians do not.

Canadians would never treat a visiting dignitary so rudely.

U.S. MUST NOT CHANNEL EUROPE ON RADICALISM
Sun-Sentinel, February 15, 2015

Re: The Front & Center interview, "CAIR leader: We decry violence."

Islamic radicalism and violence are facts, and we cannot be so politically correct as to obfuscate reality.

America must look to its future. We do not want to become like Britain, France, Norway and Sweden, where Sharia has taken over neighborhoods, where Jews live in fear and where Muslim gangs rape and prostitute children with impunity, as in Rotherham in South Yorkshire, England.

Europe is lost. It acts more and more like the Organization of Islamic Cooperation than the continent of culture, joie de vivre and freedom. The New World grew out of Europe, but we must not allow ourselves to follow its demise.

Follow-up, Orlando Sentinel: U.S. must watch for home-based terrorists.

Sunday letter-writer Len Bennett rightly and justifiably sounds the alarm to be vigilant about encroaching terrorism. He cites the attempt by radical Muslims to impose their Islamic beliefs, including their "law," on some neighbors in Europe.

He writes that we do not want to become like European countries where "Sharia has taken over neighborhoods."

He reminded me of the Ku Klux Klan takeover of neighborhoods in this country. The KKK, many espousing Christianity and carrying a cross, said, "We are the law."

The U.S. was way behind Europe when it came to ushering in racial equality.

The U.S. is closer to eradicating the remnants of the KKK legacy of intimidation, lynching, rapes, destruction of towns, corruption, take-over of law enforcement, perverted Christianity and general stupidity in this country.

We still have new anti-American terrorists of all stripes, from religious to racists to homophobes to chauvinists, residing within our country.

The Southern Poverty Law Center tracks these home-based hatemongers. According to the center, there are 939 known hate groups, including neo-Nazis, Klansmen, white nationalists, neo-Confederates, racist skinheads, black separatists and border vigilantes. There are more than 1,000 anti-government Patriot groups.

We must continue to sound the alarm against all terrorism.

CHOICE EDWARDS, CLERMONT
Exposing Palestinian Authority Evil
Haaretz, (Israel) March 4, 2015

In response to "U.S. jury finds PLO, PA liable over terror attacks in Israel more than a decade ago."

The jury in federal court in Manhattan has finally ripped the veil off the face of evil that is the Palestinian Liberation Organization and the Palestinian Authority. No more can the PA claim anything was spontaneous – not the first and second intifadas, not the attacks by rock-throwing youths who wounded and killed Israeli motorists, not the murderers who plowed vehicles into crowds at tram stops, not the thugs who stabbed unsuspecting civilians in synagogues and in the streets, and certainly not the terrorists who crept into homes at night to slaughter men, women and children.

The PA, the so-called charities that fund them, and the countries and banks which facilitate their activities are all guilty of terrorism and deserve the scorn and sanction of the civilized world.

Never again can any Islamists hide behind the façade that terror attacks were unplanned and in response to a cartoon, a video or some other perceived offense. Terror attacks in New York, Madrid, London, Benghazi, Paris and Ottawa did not just happen. They were planned. No individual or group would dare take action without the express urging and approval of their tribal rulers.

This trial has bared the truth.

NETANYAHU WON ANYWAY
Miami Herald, March 19, 2015

It looks like the Soros/Brotherhood/Obama coalition failed in their unprecedented attempt to defeat Benjamin Netanyahu in the Israeli election.

There is gnashing of teeth in the White House. There is dancing in the streets of Egypt, Jordan and Saudi Arabia.

NO ONE TO TALK TO
Haaretz, March 23, 2015

Why should it be Israel's responsibility to persuade Fatah/Hamas to come back to talks? We already know they consider everything from the Jordan River to the sea to be "occupied," want to flood Israel with 5 million so-called refugees and adamantly refuse to sign an end-of-conflict agreement.

PLO/Fatah has broken every agreement that allowed them into Ramallah to establish a Palestinian state living in peace alongside Israel. They have never eschewed terrorism and propaganda to discredit Israel and to drive out the Jews, as their brothers throughout the Arab world have done. One thing is clear. Until free nations, many bending under the strain of massive Islamic immigration and dependent on OPEC, stop groveling to the Arab League, the plan for a two-state solution will remain a pipe dream.

The Arabs could have created Palestine from 1948 to 1967, but they did not. They had no wish to. They can restart the process any time, or they can let their brothers fester in Arab-run refugee camps. Netanyahu does not need to keep proposing that the Palestinians sit down with him. He should wait until they themselves become interested. In the meantime, he has a country to protect.

Iran Hoodwinked The World
Sun-Sentinel, April 6, 2015

The preliminary agreement between Iran and the major powers guarantees Iran will be a nuclear threat. President Obama has laid the groundwork for a Middle East nuclear arms race.

The president, far from the Middle East, is crowing he rolled back Iran's bomb by 15 years, a dubious achievement even if it works. Those in the neighborhood, Saudi Arabia, Egypt and Turkey, know we've been snookered and will start their own nuclear explorations.

The so-called "powers" will free up billions of dollars the mullahs will use to expedite their designs on the West, which is to replace us with a caliphate. Iran has done a formidable job for decades. Ever since Jimmy Carter's limp noodle response to the takeover of the American Embassy, clearly an act of war, they have instigated and sponsored terrorism around the world, often using Hezbollah as their hit-men.

Fifteen years, in a conflict that has been ongoing for fifteen centuries, will pass in the blink of an eye.

The only way to roll back Iran's nuclear program is to remove its centrifuges and destroy its facilities buried underground and in mountains. That would take years to reconstitute, but is not part of the deal. In return for relief from sanctions, the Iranians are promising to 'wink-wink, nudge-nudge,' hold off nuking Israel for a few years, and that's good enough for Obama.

In a few months, he'll be out of office, put his silly little Nobel Prize on display, collect millions in consulting fees and write a few books detailing how he brought America down to size and made the United Nations the arbiter of international morality and law.

UN Biased
National Post, June 25, 2015

The United Nations is a repugnant, racist organization dominated by the 57 member states of the Organization of Islamic Cooperation. There is not one member of the OIC that even feigns a modicum of adherence to human rights. Persecution of Christians, Jews and other minorities is normal. Treating gays as pariahs and women as chattels to be bought, sold and murdered are institutionalized, while the UN remains silent. It is only Israel that merits attention.

Israel is hated for two reasons: it is the homeland of the Jews who are no longer defenseless in the face of persecution; and it is the only reliable ally of the U.S., the great Satan, loathed for its power and democracy.

Like much of the left-wing media, the report laments so few Israelis died in comparison to Gazans. That Israel protected its civilians while Hamas hid among its children is ignored. The UN will never treat Israel honestly. This report, like those before it, will be fodder for anti-Semites. Civilized society will reject it.

MIDEAST'S FUTURE IS GLOOMY
Sun-Sentinel, July 16, 2015

They're cheering in the streets of Tehran, but there is no rejoicing in Doha, Dubai, Abu Dhabi, Kuwait, Cairo, Amman, Riyadh or Jerusalem.

Iran's neighbors, like most of Europe after Chamberlain's 1938 "Peace in our times" rapprochement with Hitler, are upset and fearful. They know, as the Europeans knew, that when the major power caves in to the tyrant, the future is gloomy.

I'm sure the same reporters who crowed about the "Arab Spring" of 2010 as the beginning of a democratic Middle East are now extolling President Obama's greatest foreign policy win.

Bill Clinton's deal with North Korea in 1994 facilitated the North Korean nuclear capacity, rather than retard it. There is no doubt, Obama has helped the Iranian nuclear program and its associated terrorist activities around the globe. It will not take long to see the fallout from this agreement.

Leaving It Up To Israel
Sun-Sentinel, August 8, 2015

The West should, but will not, restrain Iran's nuclear capabilities. As America refuses to acknowledge the "clash of civilizations," it will be left to Israel to attack Iran because it is the front line and is facing the perfect storm.

Europe is overwhelmed by massive Muslim immigration and is in financial shambles. President Obama is disdainful of Israel, made an issue of settlements, rather than Arab acceptance of Israel's right to exist, and bowed to the Saudi King.

The U.S. and Europe have as much to lose as does Israel, but their governments are content to have Israel do their dirty work for them.

Unless Europe and the U.S. take dramatic steps, Israel will feel an existential threat.

Inspecting The Iran Deal: New Loopholes Discovered
New York Post, August 22, 2015

Surely, by now, there's not an American who doesn't know we've been betrayed.

By what perverted logic could the United Nations allow Iran to monitor itself?

Iran is the foremost terrorist nation in the world. Its proxies have slaughtered innocent civilians on every continent, including Americans.

Would it be beyond the pale for them to lie about what they're really using their nuclear program for?

"Death to Israel" will only take one nuclear bomb. "Death to America" will take a few more.

While Russia, China and many European countries are desperate for Iranian oil and contracts, why is this administration hell-bent on convincing itself of fantasies? This deal is a joke.

Islamic Immigration Brings Great Risks
Sun-Sentinel, September 10, 2015

Americans are a compassionate people. We want to help refugees reestablish their lives in safety, but this does not mean we have to follow Europe's lead.

In January 2013, Martin Schultz, president of the European Parliament said, "Jewish people are living in fear in Europe."

European anti-Semitism is largely the result of massive Islamic immigration. The latest rush of uncontrolled migration will further destabilize the EU and speed up the flight of Jews, particularly from the UK, France, Norway and Sweden.

We must stop calling these people "refugees." They are migrants. There is no way of knowing who is a refugee, who is an economic migrant or who is a terrorist. All are being encouraged by Arab regimes to flood Europe, while the enormously wealthy oil kings will admit no refugees into their lands. Overpopulation and the dream of a Caliphate replacing Western civilization drives the migration.

America must be cautious. Christians, Jews and other minorities, threatened by Muslims in the Middle East, North Africa and Europe, must be welcomed.

We must also demand Islamic countries take full responsibility for their own brothers. America should not be blind-sided as Europe has been.

Refugee Reservations: Major Concerns Over Safety
New York Post, September 23, 2015

Why is America so anxious to replicate the disaster unfolding in Europe?

We know 70 percent of Syrian, Iraqi, Afghani and other refugee/migrants are single draft-age men.

We also know fake Syrian passports are readily available.

No, There Will Not Be A Third Intifada
National Post, October 8, 2015

Re: Clashes Raise Prospect Of 'Third Intifada'.

There will not be a third intifada. There is no practical way for Palestinians to carry it out. This is 2015, not 2000. From 1967 to 2000 there were no demarcations between Gaza, Israel and the West Bank. Arabs, Israelis and tourists crossed back and forth to work, play and shop. The Gaza beaches were a favorite vacation spot for young Israelis. Then, after Yasser Arafat refused to sign the Clinton peace treaty, he turned loose suicide bombers to attack innocent civilians on buses, in hotels, restaurants and even at the Hebrew University of Jerusalem.

Today there is a security barrier, constructed to keep out terrorists. Like Israel's bombing of nuclear reactors in Iraq and Syria, building the barrier was a brilliant move. Terrorists will not have the easy access they had during the second intifada. As Mahmoud Abbas shreds the Oslo Accords, screams that Jews have never had a presence in Jerusalem (which also denies Christianity) and funds and glorifies murderers, he will be the big loser. A third intifada will be a civil war between Arab factions, more than an attack on Israel. Hamas and ISIL will fight for dominance, crushing the Palestinian Authority. Peaceful Arabs will caught in the cross-fire

Who Is Best For The Jews?
Canadian Jewish News, October 10, 2015

Canadian Jews are not one-issue voters. Jews are educated and sophisticated and are passionate about human rights and a prosperous, safe and secure Canada.

While the major parties have expressed support for Israel during this election campaign, their past actions are more revealing. The Conservatives have always been solid supporters of Israel's right to exist peacefully, while the Liberal and NDP parties have not. From participating in the Durban conference and seldom voting against anti-

Israel resolutions at the UN, Liberal support has been lukewarm at best. There is a Diefenbaker Forest in Israel, not one named after Pearson.

For the last hundred years, Jews have blindly voted Liberal. Those days are over. Like it or not, the Middle East is a partisan issue, with the Conservatives seeking Jewish votes and the Liberals and NDP courting the Muslims, though the Liberal foreign and immigration policies have these votes in the bag.

MIDDLE EAST PEACE
Miami Herald, November 7, 2015

Yitzhak Rabin, like Ehud Barak and Benjamin Netanyahu, was a warrior who wanted peace. On the other side, Yasser Arafat, like Mahmoud Abbas, was a con man who used the Oslo Accords to gain an advantage in the plan to eliminate the Jewish state.

The Oslo talks were launched by Shimon Peres behind Rabin's back. Rabin, trapped by Peres and Clinton, signed the Accords with the man who rose to fame by terrorism and who started civil wars in Jordan and Lebanon. Rabin wasn't so naive as to think Arafat had changed. Arafat took the land and the money and refused to implement even the first step, which was to stop incitement to violence.

Rabin's murderer did not derail the peace effort. In 2000, the Clinton-Barak-Arafat peace talks gave Arafat everything he claimed to want, but he would not sign an "end of conflict" statement. Instead he launched suicide bombers against innocent Israeli civilians, Jews and Arabs on buses and in hotels, restaurants and clubs. His intifada terrorized Israelis, hurt their economy, destroyed the economy in the disputed territories and ended the relaxed co-existence between Israelis and Palestinian Arabs.

Had Rabin lived, he would likely have called out Arafat for the fraud he was. Perhaps, with Clinton's support, Arafat's PLO/PA could have been replaced with a leadership that wanted peace.

KEYSTONE PIPE DREAMS
New York Post, October 15, 2015

That didn't take long.

Only four days into the new Canadian government, Prime Minister Justin Trudeau and Obama have traded opening shots.

Canada announced it was pulling out of the fight against ISIS, and the US announced it was rejecting the pipeline.

The losers include North America's economy and the Christians, Yazidis and Kurds trapped in the Syrian civil war. The winners are Saudi Arabia and OPEC.

FLAWED ASSESSMENT
Jerusalem Post, December 10, 2015

US President Barack Obama's assessment of Muslims attitudes towards others is faulty and this will have a negative and unalterable impact on our liberal societies as Muslims migrate across Europe and North America ("In rare Oval Office address, Obama warns of new phase of terrorism," December 8).

Since French leader Charles de Gaulle turned his back on Israel and invited Islamic immigration, Muslims have set up 750 no-go zones in France, where sharia is the only law. Violence against infidels, and particularly against Jews, is rampant and goes largely unpunished, as authorities fear being targeted as Islamophobes.

Jews are leaving Europe in record numbers. Two years ago, Martin Schultz, president of the European Union Parliament said, "Jewish people are living in fear." In November, Rabbi Avraham Gigi, chief rabbi of Belgium said, "There is no future for Jews in Europe."

In just about every Western university the Muslim Students' Associations, which, like Hamas, is the progeny of the Muslim Brotherhood, promotes the racist boycott, divestment and sanctions and the Israel Apartheid week movements.

The correlation is obvious. Western anti-Semitism is growing in direct proportion to Muslim immigration.

If history has taught us anything, it is that the Jew is the canary in the coal mine.

Anti-Semitism On The Rise
National Post, December 29, 2015

Re: Germany's Redemption, Roger Cohen.

Does Roger Cohen not see the irony of linking German Chancellor Angela Merkel, refugees and Jews together? The truth is that, as the level of Muslim immigration rises, so does anti-Semitism.

Following the 1973 oil crises, France and the Arab League restructured the Euro-Arab relationship to the detriment of America and Israel. Muslims have since set up 750 "no-go" zones in France where sharia is the law. The same has been replicated throughout Europe. Violence against infidels, and particularly against Jews, is rampant and goes largely unpunished.

So while Cohen lauds "Merkel's place in the history books," and millions of refugees, economic migrants and jihadists flow into Europe, Europeans will again be searching for a safe haven.

"Everyone thinks of changing
the world, but no one thinks of
changing himself." —Leo Tolstoy

2016

TIME FOR ALL NATIONS TO RETHINK IMMIGRATION
Sun-Sentinel, January 4, 2016

The threat to European society is not multiculturalism or xenophobia, but rather the type of immigrants they are accepting.

Immigrants to Europe must adapt to Europe, not demand that host countries acquiesce to their wishes to replicate their old lives, even to Europe's detriment.

When my grandparents immigrated to Canada 101 years ago, they kissed the ground. They were grateful to Canada for freeing them from oppression, for giving them a fresh start and they tried to fit into the Canadian way of life. They would never have thought to demand special treatment. They were proud Canadians. Their religion was a private matter, not one that public institutions had to bend to.

Muslim emigration to the West has been troublesome. The majority appear not to want to join the mainstream of their adopted countries, but to replicate their cultures and conflicts and to establish enclaves where Sharia law over-rides the law of the land.

In England, France, Sweden and Norway, Jews fear for their safety and are leaving in record numbers.

In Western universities, Jewish students are harassed by the Muslim Brotherhood-controlled 'Israel Apartheid Week' and 'Boycott, Divest and Sanction' anti-Israel/anti-Semitic groups.

We must all rethink our immigration policies. We need immigrants who want to become part of their chosen country, not one's who want to dominate.

BAN'S WORDS
Jerusalem Post, January 28, 2016

There is nothing Israel can do to prevent terrorism. Terrorism has its own agenda. Israelis are not provoking it by either their actions or non-actions.

Islamic terrorism is opportunistic. Its goal is the destruction of Western societies and their replacement with a caliphate. Radical Islam has the Koran, the mosque and the media to propel it. It doesn't need us.

Today, as we see the invasion of Europe and the lap-dog eagerness of Western companies and governments to do business with Iran, one has to wonder why terrorism is required at all, unless it's just one more element to speed the fall of the Judeo-Christian world.

FRENCH FRAME-UP OF ISRAEL
Haaretz, February 2, 2016

What duplicity. France has already prejudged the outcome of its proposed conference on the Arab-Israeli conflict. It has predetermined that Israel would be at fault if an agreement is not reached, and France would recognize a Palestinian state.

What incentive do the Arabs have to reach an agreement with Israel? They can demand that all of Jerusalem be their capital, that 5 million Arabs be admitted into Israel and that Islam becomes the state religion of Israel.

They have nothing to lose. One way or another, France will recognize them, just as Iceland, Sweden and the Vatican have. It will further delegitimize Israel and support the Arab claim that Israel must be dismantled.

It is little wonder French Jews are leaving in record numbers. Fortunately, Israel and Quebec will welcome and protect them.

NEED TO BREAK THE CYCLE
National Post, February 3, 2016

"'Balance' over 'fairness' " is news-speak for supporting Arabs at the expense of Jews. Liberal governments have never been "a steadfast ally and friend to Israel." That role was exclusively a Conservative one.

Foreign Minister Stéphane Dion hardly rapped the knuckles of the Arab who stabbed an 80-year old Israeli grandmother. He doesn't comment on three months of Islamic terrorism against Israelis. He accepts as normal the 28 dead and 280 injured Jews in 22 car rammings, 37 shootings and 105 knife attacks in the first three month of Palestinian Authority/Hamas/Islamic State of Iraq and the Levant-inspired violence. It is Israel he chastises for building apartments in areas he knows will be in Israeli territory if there ever is an Arab-Israeli peace deal. It is Israel he warns against defending itself.

It won't take much longer for Jewish voters to question their unblinking support for the Liberal party. As hundreds of thousands of Muslims flood into Canada in the next four years, the Jewish vote will be irrelevant.

OBAMA PREACHING TOLERANCE
New York Post, February 5, 2016

Where is the president's concern for American Jews?
Why the double standard when there's so much anti-Semitism?

RETROACTIVELY PALESTINIAN
Jerusalem Post, March 18, 2016

The word "Palestinian" is thrown around gratuitously, with few knowing what they're talking about.

Until 1920, there was no place called Palestine and hence, no Palestinian people.

In 1918, following World War One, Turkey lost the Ottoman Empire it occupied since 1299. The allies carved it up as per the Sykes-Picot Agreement, creating boundaries for favored chieftains and leaving little areas for Christians (Lebanon) and Jews (Palestine). The Brits immediately gave away 80% of Palestine to create Trans Jordan. Till then there were no Palestinians.

The region was sparsely populated by Muslims, Christians, Jews and others. As Zionists began migrating in the 1880's, Arabs from neighboring countries followed for two reasons. They moved for the employment the Jews created and were also encouraged to do so to limit the building of large Jewish settlements.

From then until 1948, only Jews were called "Palestinians." Everyone else was an Egyptian, Syria or an Arab of another origin. There was no 'Palestinian culture.'

There was the Palestine Post, the Anglo-Palestine Bank, The Palestine Electric Company and the Palestine Symphony; all Jewish organizations, run by Jews.

In 1964, the KGB and Egypt created the PLO, mandated to liberate Palestine from the Jews through armed struggle.

Palestinian Arabs were now referred to as Palestinians, however, to retroactively define pre-1964 Arabs as Palestinians is to feed the narrative that Jews have no attachment to Palestine or Israel or Jerusalem.

THE BDS FLOP
Jerusalem Post, March 23, 2016

Regarding the news item that British Secretary of Justice Michael Graves came out against the BDS movement (News in brief), the boycott, divestment and sanctions (BDS) movement is racism, pure and simple.

It is one tentacle of the Muslim Brotherhood, the epicenter for Sunni terrorism. There is a straight line from the Brotherhood to CAIR (Congress of American Islamic Relations), MSA (Muslim Students' Association), Hamas and ISIS. It is the source from which al-Qaeda sprang.

The Brotherhood created CAIR to infiltrate Western militaries and governments and MSA to influence our education system. The movement to boycott Israel shows the power of the MSA. Hamas is the MB's Middle East wing.

Saudis and the gulf sheikdoms have funded chairs in all our universities. Those teaching these classes must skew lectures to show Islam in a favorable light in contract to decadent Western, Christian and other philosophies.

Israeli Arabs are the best educated and the most free in the Middle East and North Africa. They make up 19% of Israel's medical school students. They are 20% of Israeli doctors and pharmacists and 25% of its nurses. An Arab sits on Israel's Supreme Court and the Arab Joint List is the third largest block in the Knesset.

Israel is the one Mideast haven where gays, Christians, Baha'i, Bedouin and Africans can flee to escape persecution throughout the Arab world. Israel's neighbors hang gays, murder infidels, defile and torch churches, treat their woman as chattels, keep slaves and have confined Palestinian Arab refugees in UN welfare camps in Gaza, the West Bank, Lebanon, Syria and Jordan for generations.

Israel is an economic and scientific dynamo. It has relations and trades with most of the world. Its growth is a magnet for investment. If forced to move factories from the disputed territories, thousands of Arabs will lose high-paying jobs. Is that what BDS wants? Whoever divests from Israel will find others eager to snap up their stocks. The net effect on Israel's economy will be zero.

Aside from the propaganda value, BDS has been a flop. If its aim is the destruction of Israel, then all discussion is moot. If the goal is a Palestinian Arab state living in peace alongside Israel, the answer is for the Arab League to stop incitement and to accept a Jewish neighbor.

AMERICA AND THE SAUDIS: TIME FOR A BREAKUP?
New York Post, April 20, 2016

It's about time we realized that Saudi Arabia is not a longtime US ally. It has nothing in common with our values.

The Saudi government is against everything we cherish. It's anti-freedom of speech and religion, anti-equality under the law and anti-human rights.

It's a one-family-controlled country that has contributed nothing to society, aside from funding chairs in our universities as propaganda for its agenda.

ANTI-SEMITISM ON CAMPUS
National Post, April 28, 2016

Re: Don't Blame The Media For Islamophobia.

Jonathan Kay is way off base on anti-Semitism. He has obviously not spent much time talking to Jewish students in many of our universities. They are bombarded by racism generated by the Muslim students' associations and their boycott, divest and sanction (BDS) and Israel Apartheid Week movements. They are further harassed by left-wing professors.

UNCONSCIONABLE FOR GERMANY TO ALLOW 'MEIN KAMPF' TO RESURFACE
Boston Globe, May 11, 2016

In my opinion, there is only one reason to carry "Mein Kampf" on any library shelf, and that is pure, unadulterated racism ("Keeping 'Mein Kampf' in print"). The book has been a bestseller throughout the Islamic world, but it is unconscionable for Germany, the country responsible for the deaths of 6 million Jews, to allow it to resurface.

As for serious American and German historians, and the Munich Institute of Contemporary History, who are supporting an annotated edition, my comment is, "Shame."

A SUMMER OF TRUMP
Canadian Jewish News, June 9, 2016

Donald Trump understands that the more left-wing a person is – be they American or Israeli, Muslim, Christian, Jew or atheist – the more likely they are to be anti-American and anti-Semitic ("Liberal Jews plan a summer of opposing Donald Trump").

For decades, Americans and the U.S. Congress have supported Israel, but their leaders have blown hot and cold. While everyone loved former U.S. president Bill Clinton's charm, he was of another, gentler era. Following 9/11, then-president George Bush had a much tougher and more violent world to contend with, and the administration of President Barack Obama and former secretary of state Hillary Clinton was a disaster for the Middle East. They genuflected to the oil tyrants and acquiesced to their demand that Israel be the price for Arab co-operation. Meanwhile, Obama/Clinton left the Middle East and North Africa in flames, with only Israel managing to stay above the fray.

Trump's balance on Arab-Israeli issues will be a welcome change from Obama's stance. Americans should know Hillary Clinton will be more of the same, and Saudi funds will continue to pour into the Clinton Foundation.

For generations, Democrats have taken Jewish votes for granted. That is over. Those supporting Israelis' right to live in peace in their ancestral homeland will gravitate toward the conservatives they trust, rather than the wishy-washy progressives who parrot the mantra that all cultures are equal to ours and that Islamic human rights will fall into place if only we treated them better.

ARAB LEAGUE THE KEY
Jerusalem Post, June 14, 2016

With regard to "De-risking peace – part 2," progress toward a Palestinian state is still possible if the Arab League is interested in one.

It is not Israel that holds the cards. As the Arab goal for the past hundred years has been to drive the Jews into the sea, perhaps the concept of two separate states, a Jewish one with a large Arab minority, and an Arab one that is ethnically cleansed of Jews, is no longer feasible.

From 1967 to 2000, there were no demarcation lines between the Gaza Strip, Israel and Judea and Samaria. Israelis and Arabs crossed back and forth freely. Trade schools and universities were built in the former Egyptian and Jordanian-occupied areas where none had existed before. Electricity usage grew. Infant mortality rates declined. The standard of living rose.

Perhaps the answer lies somewhere between a bi-national state and two totally separate states. Perhaps a confederation, with separate civil administrations, an Israeli military and joint policing and economic cooperation. This presupposes, of course, that the Arab League would allow an infidel entity to share the Middle East.

WAKING UP TO THE JIHADIST THREAT
New York Daily News, June 14, 2016

Another terrorist attack on America by a Muslim. Of course, his father says it has nothing to do with his religion. He just hated gays.

Did he get his inspiration from his brothers in Hamas who throw gays off rooftops? Was he emulating the murders and hangings of gays throughout the Islamic world?

At least 49 Americans are dead and more wounded because of a man adhering to a supremacist radical ideology that promotes the slaying of infidels in the name of Allah.

It matters if Mateen was, or was not, linked to a terrorist organization. But what is more relevant is the easy accessibility to violent teachings in mosques, schools, media and the internet. Even our universities have been polluted by the left-wing agenda of professors holding chairs funded by the Saudis and Gulf kingdoms and the Muslim Students' Association. Mass Islamic immigration breeds terrorism. We must learn from the European experience.

ISRAEL IS NOT AN 'APARTHEID' STATE
Irish Independent, June 15, 2016

In response to the letter 'Boycott is a legitimate response to regime's apartheid,' Judea and Samaria (West Bank) is "disputed", not "occupied" territory. Palestine is not, nor has it ever been, a country. It was part of the Ottoman Empire and then a British Mandate, but never a country.

It was a potential country in 1948, but the Arabs refused the UN Partition Plan and Egypt and Jordan took over Gaza and the West Bank. Israel captured the territories in the 1967 war of genocide against the Jews. To use the term "apartheid" is an insult to both South Africans and Israelis.

In Israel and the territories, Muslims and Christians have control of their holy places, unlike 1948-1967, when Jews were forced out of the West Bank and Gaza and were barred from entering.

In Israel, all citizens have equal rights. There are Arab parties and members in the Knesset. There are Arab judges and one is on the Supreme Court. There are Arab professors and students in all universities, and Arab doctors and patients in all hospitals.

Any comparison of Israel with South Africa is ignorance or bigotry.

JNF AND THE GREENS
National Post, July 20, 2016

BDS is one of the anti- Semitic movements pledged to destroy the state of Israel. It has nothing to do with supposed injustices done to the Arabs. The Green Party is supposed to care about the environment and preserving the earth. How can its members try to take away the charitable status of the JNF, the most successful ecological organization in the world? Israel is the only country that left the 20th century with more trees than 100 years before. Why are they not applauding this unique achievement? I am left with the impression that racism is more their platform than being "green." As a Canadian, I am disgusted.

TRUMP & CLINTON
Boston Globe, August 3, 2016

Re: Republicans in Congress distance selves from Trump comments.

Republicans are missing the full context of this story.

Of course, Donald Trump was stupid for falling for the bait the Clinton campaign set for him. There are few things so touching as parents grieving a child lost in war. Soldiers of every ethnicity died, but Hillary Clinton and the Democrats chose a Muslim family to make a point, and had them attack Trump, which was unconscionable. The Khans should not have been political foils.

Both Clinton and Trump should be ashamed of themselves, but in this election, common decency is in short supply.

Trump Has Right Idea On Immigration Policy
USA Today, August 21, 2016

Donald Trump understands that the threat to American society is not multiculturalism, but rather the type of immigrants we accept.

Muslim emigration to the West has been troublesome. The majority will not join the mainstream of their adopted countries, but replicate their cultures and conflicts and establish enclaves where Sharia law over-rides the law of the land.

We need only look to the Islamic invasion of Europe. Immigrants, whether refugees, economic migrants or terrorists, have not adapted. They are attracted by overly-generous welfare systems and will cause economic chaos.

In Britain, for example, the Islamic Emirates Project named territories to be targeted for blanket Sharia rule.

In France, there are areas where those who enter must conform to Islamic norms. In England, France, Sweden and Norway, Jews fear for their safety and are leaving in record numbers.

In our universities, Jewish students are harassed by the Muslim student groups.

Trump knows we must rethink our immigration policies.

Coerced To Cover Up
National Post, August 26, 2016

Re: Burkini Bans Could Face Legal Challenge.

The burkini is just the current issue in the cultural conflict exacerbated by the Islamic invasion of Europe. The mothers and grandmothers of the women who now cover up dressed in modern clothing in most of the Middle

East 50 years ago, before religious suppression took hold. Egyptian, Iranian and Turkish women were very chic. Beirut was "the Paris of the East."

There are two main reasons women wear the hijab, burka, abaya, niqab chador or burkini. The first is coercion by families and imams. The women fear for their place in society and for their personal safety. The second advances the jihad. It says we are here, we are in charge and we are taking over.

The suppression, domination and coercion of Islamic women and the role they are forced to play are what this discussion should be about.

DEFENDING TERROR
New York Daily News, September 5, 2016
Voice Of The People

Let's be perfectly clear about this. Americans were murdered by Palestinian terrorists. After many years waiting for the American government to take action, the families sued in federal court and won a $655 million civil judgment. Instead of allowing justice to proceed, the Obama government intervened, warning that the case "threatened to financially destabilize the Palestinian government." The 2nd U.S. Circuit Court of Appeals in Manhattan overruled the lower court. The bottom line is that if Palestinian terrorists murder Americans overseas, it's OK with this government.

UNAPPEALING SCENARIO
Jerusalem Post, September 8, 2016

With regard to "Most support referendum on two states," who funds these anti-Israel NGOs that keep popping up? This one seems to have no function other than propaganda.

Legally, the disputed territories are neither Palestinian nor occupied. Second, there is nothing new to be learned from yet another survey in Israel, Gaza or Judea and Samaria. The Jews accepted the 1947 UN plan to create a Jewish and an Arab state. The Arabs rejected it. Nothing has changed in the intervening years.

Were Israel to scrap the Oslo Accords and leave the territories to the Palestinian Authority, as it did in the Gaza Strip, the same thing would occur: Arabs would die in the fight for control between Fatah and Hamas, but this time with Hezbollah and Islamic State eventually joining in. To gain street cred, they'd all lob rockets into Israel and launch terrorism against it and each other.

No Arab faction will allow Israel to exist in any borders. Only the Arab League can bring about change, but it won't so long as a wishy-washy American administration panders to it.

READERS REFLECT ON THE LEGACY OF
SHIMON PERES
Jerusalem Post, October 4, 2016

Shimon Peres's major error was signing the Oslo Accords with Yasser Arafat instead of waiting for an Arab leader interested in living alongside a Jewish state.

Arafat killed the possibility of peace by planning his intifada before the Camp David summit with Ehud Barak. The proposal gave the Arabs everything they claimed to want, except for one crucial element – it included an end-of-conflict statement, which Arafat could not accept.

He made it clear he would not bind the next generation's right to revisit the situation. So he turned suicide bombers loose on Israeli civilians because he had always succeeded with terrorism and knew no other mode of diplomacy.

Palestinian Arabs have been hostage to their Arab neighbors for the past 100 years, and only they can set themselves free.

Another Echo
Miami Herald, October 12, 2016

Alan Berger's article has one thing right and everything else wrong.

Europe today is an echo of the 1930s, but Jihadists are driving the agenda this time and Jews are again fleeing. Just as large numbers of left-wing Nazi supporters in Europe and America either cooperated with, or stood by and did nothing, progressives today are facilitating Islam's goal of destroying Western democracy and replacing it with a caliphate.

It is not Donald Trump's pushback against Islamic migration that is the problem, but rather Georges Soros and the Muslim Brotherhood, entwined with the Obama/Clinton administration.

Successive American administrations welcomed the Brotherhood's input, reasoning they were not as bad as al-Qaida. They were wrong. The Muslim Brotherhood is the epicenter of Sunni terrorism world-wide.

Europe and America are under attack by radical Islam. As in the 1930s, Jews are its first victims, but the "Great Satan" is the prize. The Obama/Clinton ties to the Brotherhood and Gulf princes are many and complex.

UNESCO's Shame
National Post, October 22, 2016

Re: *An Attack On Both Our Houses, Shimon Koffler Fogel.*

Once again we have looked into the face of evil. Twenty-four members of UNESCO have committed genocide on truth. They have denied the 4,000-year history of the Jewish people and their attachment to Israel. They denied the 3,000-year history of Jerusalem, which housed King Solomon's Temple. They denied that 2,000 years ago, the Second Temple sat atop the Temple Mount and was destroyed by the Romans in 71 AD. If there was no Temple, there was no Christ.

Twenty-six members of this paragon of evil abstained; each one a coward.

Every Islamic member of UNESCO voted in favor, elucidating triumphantly that Judaism and Christianity will be subjugated

TRUDEAU, CLINTON ARE TWO OF A KIND
Ottawa Citizen, November 15, 2016

Liberals and Democrats selected their newest leaders the same way. Insiders anointed known names. It would have been a cozy relationship for Justin Trudeau if Hillary Clinton had won. Both would have followed Europe's lead with open borders, free trade and unfettered Muslim immigration.

America opted for sovereignty over globalization, just as Britain has. Other European Union members will follow suit and wrest decision-making from the unelected Brussels bureaucrats.

On the plus side, North American energy can now expand and OPEC's power will diminish. Climate change will take a back seat to the economy and foreign and domestic policies in the U.S., issues that went awry during the Obama years.

Canada's Liberal practices will distance us from our closest neighbor and partner. Aside from trade, security considerations may well become prominent.

OBAMA'S GOODBYE
Miami Herald, November 26, 2016

One would hope President Obama will use his last few weeks in office to visit the world, make his goodbyes and pave the way for his role as a global statesman.

The United States has not had much success in the Middle East. Bill Clinton failed to get Yasser Arafat to agree on peace. George Bush pushed for Palestinian Authority elections and Hamas took over Gaza. Obama prematurely pulled out of Iraq and ISIL moved in. He attacked Libya with awful consequences. Attempts to solve the Arab-Israeli conflict failed as well.

The Oslo accords, which allowed the PLO into Israel, dictate that Israel and the PA would negotiate the details of peace between themselves. That should not be tampered with.

UN PROTECTION
Jerusalem Post, December 7, 2016

With regard to "UNGA passes six votes condemning Israel, again," the Palestinians, as a people, were created in 1964 when the KGB and Egypt set up the PLO to drive the Jews out of Israel.

From the start of the British Mandate for Palestine until 1948, only local Jews referred to themselves as Palestinians. Arabs identified with their countries of origin: They were Egyptians, Syrians, etc. According to "The Smoking Gun: Arab Immigration into Palestine, 1922-1931" by Fred M. Gottheil (Middle East Quarterly, Winter 2003), most migrated to Palestine in the 1920s and 30s at the encouragement of their leaders and to find employment.

The PLO refined terrorism as a means of diplomacy. It invented airplane hijacking for political purposes and was successful in projecting its cause onto the world stage.

Suicide bombings and vehicles ramming into crowds are more recent innovations, as are arson and knife attacks. These modes of destruction are now standard Islamist terror methods used internationally. In addition, the BDS movement and claims of Israeli "apartheid" are Palestine's way of harassing Jewish university students.

For these achievements, the Palestinians are protected by the United Nations.

THE U.S. FAILED ISRAEL ON THE INTERNATIONAL STAGE
USA Today, December 26, 2016

Dec. 23, 2016 will be marked down as a day of infamy. President Barack Obama betrayed America and Israel. The U.S.'s abstention on the measure to cease Israeli settlements at the United Nations Security Council will be Obama's legacy.

The 14 members who voted against the only free country in the Middle East — a country where Jews, Muslims and Christians are equal under the law — are pathetic.

Out of those who voted in favor of the measure, democratic countries like the United Kingdom and France are cowed by their terror-prone Muslim immigrants. On the other hand, New Zealand, one of the sponsors of the resolution, seems to have adopted anti-Israel policies in recent years. The others are all Muslim dictatorships or failed states, where human rights are non-existent.

Not one of the 14 can compare with Israel's technological or intellectual successes, in my opinion. Shame on them all.

2017

ISRAEL OUTRAGE
Dominion Post New Zealand, January 7, 2017

Israel is not "irked" by New Zealand joining three dictatorships and sponsoring the UN Security Council resolution. It is outraged that another small democracy would do this.

The concept of Israel taking military or cyber action against New Zealand is just plain silly.

What will hurt New Zealand is the loss of technical co-operation with the greatest concentration of brain-power in the world. Israel is tiny compared to New Zealand. It has twice the population. It has 12 Nobel Prizes. How many has New Zealand won?

While your economy is agriculture, Israeli technology is in billions of pockets, homes and offices.

Surely, Israeli bedroom communities on 3 per cent of the disputed territories was not what "irked" you.

NO PARALLEL BETWEEN HOLOCAUST VICTIMS AND MUSLIM REFUGEES
Haaretz, January 30, 2017

Regarding "ADL chief: History will frown on Trump's heartless attack on refugees" (Jonathan Greenblatt.)

Greenblatt's op-ed is bigotry. Why would he link today's Muslim refugees/migrants with the victims of the Holocaust? Anti-Semitism is the world's longest-lasting sin, driven in the 20th and 21st centuries by the union of Nazism and radical Islam.

From the late 1920s, the British-appointed Grand Mufti of Jerusalem, Haj Amin al-Husseini, persecuted the Jews of the British Mandate. He was involved in organizing and recruiting Muslims into the mainly Bosnian-Muslim 13th Waffen Mountain Division of the SS Handschar, and he and Hitler had plans to follow Rommel's forces into Palestine to continue the Holocaust.

The greatest source of anti-Semitism today is Islam, whether one looks at the United Nations or other international bodies. Brought to their knees in the early 1970s by the Arab oil embargo, most nations abandoned Israel and played into the Islamists' agenda.

In America, the Muslim Brotherhood, the epicenter for Sunni terrorism, had made great strides. Its surrogates are Hamas, the Council on American–Islamic Relations and the Muslim Students Association. CAIR is tasked with infiltrating their government and military. The MSA brings anti-Semitism to universities with Israel Apartheid Week, the boycott, divestment and sanctions movement and other so-called pro-Palestinian actions. Hamas, of course, is mandated to kill Jews everywhere.

By all means, link anti-Semitism with other atrocities, but the United States, like Europe, has paid a price for allowing unvetted immigration. There are 56 Islamic nations that could/should take care of their brothers.

EMBASSY IN JERUSALEM
Jerusalem Post, January 30, 2017

The caterwauling about the dire consequences of moving the US Embassy to Jerusalem ("Erekat: We'll counter Jerusalem embassy move,") is the height of hypocrisy. If Israel annexes major Jewish towns that make up 2% of the disputed territories, or the US builds a new embassy on a lot in Jerusalem it purchased in the 1990s, nothing will change.

If the new Trump administration treats all sides of the Arab-Israeli conflict equally and has the same expectation for both Arabs and Jews, he might effect a calmer environment in the short term.

JVP Conference
Jerusalem Post, February 3, 2017

With regard to "Jewish Voice for Peace 'honored, proud' to host confessed terrorist Odeh," Jewish Voice for Peace is anti-Semitic. How else could one explain the group's outrage against Israel while every one of Israel's neighbors is blatantly apartheid in their treatment of women, gays, Christians and other infidels?

Israel is the only safe haven for Christians, Bedouin, Baha'is and others fleeing persecution in the Middle East and North Africa. Israeli Arabs have more rights and freedom than any other Arabs.

Israel defended itself from Arab aggression in three wars of genocide against the Jews (1948, 1967 and 1973.) Had it lost any of these wars, its people would have been slaughtered.

Israel has no control over the human rights of Palestinians. Fatah controls the lives of 95% of West Bank Arabs. Hamas runs Gaza. Arabs have kept Palestinian refugees in fetid camps in Gaza, the West Bank, Lebanon, Syria and Jordan since 1948, controlled by UNRWA and the Arab League. They are the cause of Palestinian suffering.

Israeli Arabs have the same rights and responsibilities as other Israelis. The make up 19% of medical school students. Twenty percent of Israeli doctors and pharmacists are Arabs, as are 25% of the country's nurses.

Racism is the disproportionate criticism of one party while giving its adversaries a pass.

Readers React To Sentencing Of Elor Azaria
Jerusalem Post, February 24, 2017

Elor Azaria was tried and convicted, and is going to jail. In contrast, the Palestinian Authority names parks and schools in honor of people who kill Jews, and the murderers and their families receive pensions for life with funds provided by American taxpayers and the EU.

Hollywood 'Moonlight' Madness
New York Daily News, February 28, 2017

Wrong messenger.

The Academy Awards are meant to display cleavage, make far-left statements and reward excellence in film making. They did not disappoint. However, the irony of Iranians, whose country is the world's main supporter of terrorism, lecturing the United States and getting a prolonged ovation from the glitterati made me gag on my Cristal.

Islam And Our Judeo-Christian Heritage
Haaretz, April 10, 2017

In regard to "Jews Pay the Price When 'Judeo-Christian Values' Are on Sale," we should be asking when and why we decided to replace our Judeo-Christian heritage with Islam, a belief system that holds little in common with Western liberal thought.

For all of its 1,400-year history, Islam has taught subjugation of infidels in the vast territories it conquered and colonized.

We forget that Haj Amin al-Husseini, the Grand Mufti of Jerusalem, was Hitler's ally. He directed attacks against British Mandate troops and pogroms against the Jews of Palestine and Iraq.

After World War II, the Middle East and North Africa rejected all Christian and Jewish rights and history. Seven hundred thousand Christians were forced out of Lebanon by the Palestine Liberation Organization's civil war and 850,000 Jews were evicted from the region. The PLO displaced 80% of Bethlehem's Christians.

Europe is in trouble. Sharia law has replaced European law in hundreds of neighborhoods.

Who voted for this?

Dems Must Get Smart
Miami Herald, May 2, 2017

Re: Democrats say they now know exactly why Clinton lost.

Hillary Clinton lost the presidential race because Democrats refused to cut with the past. If they stay the course, they will lose the mid-terms and the 2020 elections as well.

The Soros/Obama/Clinton troika continues to dominate the party. The corruption and left-wing politics they followed for eight years have weakened America and hurt the party.

In 2016, Americans rejected open borders, Islamism and pay-for play. In their hearts, Americans believe they are a great nation. They see how freedom and safety are being undermined in Europe. They see the effect of open borders, mass Muslim migration, no-go zones and Sharia law — and they don't want it replicated here.

So long as the Soros/Obama/Clinton team won't leave the stage, Democrats will be seen as the party obsessed with ruining President Trump, regardless of the cost. That's not good enough.

Breaking The Silence NGO Not A Reliable Source
Sun-Sentinel, May 7, 2017

The largely foreign-funded Israeli NGO Breaking the Silence is not a reliable source of information. They have an anti-Israel, anti-military agenda. They employ unsubstantiated anecdotal stories to promote their program.

The group was launched after the last Hamas-Israel conflict. Their casting of Israel's rules of engagement as negative, while Hamas executes spies on television — and the United Nations admitted three of its posts were Hamas war facilities — should eliminate any shred of belief in them.

With a 1 to 1 civilian to military death count, Israel is recognized as the most humane army in the world, phoning, texting and dropping leaflets warning the population, including militants, of impending action. The normal ratio is 3 or 4 to 1 in all other conflicts.

Criticize Israel if you choose, but Breaking the Silence is hate-mongering. The German foreign minister should know better.

GLAVIN WRONG ON TRUMP'S VISIT TO MIDDLE EAST
Ottawa Citizen, May 20, 2017

Re: The last thing we need: Trump's visit to Israel.

Terry Glavin is wrong. Where better for the leader of the free world's first foreign foray than to the heart of Judaism, Jerusalem and to the leaders of the two major religions that sprang from it?

Israel is the eighth most powerful country on Earth and sits in the middle of the volatile Middle East and North Africa.

Saudi Arabia gave us the oil embargo in the 1970s that brought Europe to its knees and forced it to forgo its Judeo-Christian heritage. It gave birth to al-Qaida and supports terrorist organizations worldwide.

Israel and Saudi Arabia are the only powers that can influence the Arab-Israeli conflict.

UN USELESS
Jerusalem Post, June 9, 2017

UN Secretary-General Antonio Guterres recently said Israel's 50 years of occupation has imposed a "heavy humanitarian and development burden on the Palestinian people" and "fueled recurring cycles of violence and retribution."

He knows that had Israel lost to Egypt, Jordan and Syria in 1967, there would have been no "Israeli occupation." The Jews would have been slaughtered and the victors would have divided the land. The Palestinian Arabs, never called "Palestinians" until the KGB and Egypt invented the PLO in 1964, would have continued to be part of the Arab world. There would have been no further talk of "Palestine."

Genocide has been the declared goal of the Arabs from 1948 to this day. They are still fighting World War II. They were allied with Hitler, participated in the Holocaust and will not accept an infidel entity in their midst.

The term "Palestinian leadership" is a non sequitur. It doesn't exist. The Palestinian Authority sees a three-state solution. Its president, Mahmoud Abbas, knows he cannot win against Hamas. He envisions Hamas controlling the Gaza Strip, the PA controlling a Jew-free West Bank, and an Israel that is a multi-ethnic society where anyone claiming a Palestinian linkage could immigrate to. Hamas sees one Islamic caliphate, free of infidels – including the PA.

Propaganda terminology such as "apartheid," "occupation," "Palestinian territories" and "oppression" notwithstanding, there is nothing Israel can offer to entice the Palestinian leadership to cooperate.

Only Saudi Arabia and the US have the power to influence an outcome to the conflict. Perhaps with newly-gained confidence that the US has their back vis-a-vis Iran, the Saudis could play a positive role. The UN is useless.

UNESCO's Move
Jerusalem Post, July 11, 2017

With regard to "Israel cuts funding to protest UNESCO decision on Hebron," the Tomb of the Patriarchs is the burial site of the first Jews. This surely defines it as a Jewish site.

Centuries later, Muhammad found refuge among the Jews of Medina when he was forced out of Mecca. He learned about their beliefs and stories, and adopted many of them as his own. Then he beheaded the men and boys, took the women as slaves and launched his jihad across the Middle East and the world. This might give Muslims a claim to the site. However, calling it "Palestinian" stretches all credulity.

The notion of a people called "the Palestinians" was invented in 1964 when the KGB and Egypt founded the PLO. The purpose of the PLO was to drive out the Jews. During the period of the British Mandate for Palestine, only Jews were called Palestinians. Many of the Arabs of Palestine were recent immigrants from surrounding countries and identified themselves as Egyptians, Syrians, etc. At the UN partition talks, the Syrian ambassador said there was no such thing as Palestine. Ultimately, the UN defined an Arab Palestinian refugee as anyone who lived in the area for two years.

The United Nations is an unabashedly anti-Semitic organization, dominated by the demands of the 57-member Organization of Islamic Cooperation. Israel, the only shining light in the Middle East, is the excuse for the violence and corruption that is the Islamic world.

That UNESCO sees Israel as its whipping boy is repugnant and ordinary. That the West still pretends the UN has value doesn't bode well for democracy.

It's The Arab Hatred, Stupid
New York Daily News, July 26, 2017

This is another iteration of the 100-year old "Al-Aqsa libel." ("UN urges resolution of Jerusalem shrine crisis,") Its function was/is to distract the peasants' attention away from their own corrupt and inept leadership and to focus blame for their miserable lives on the Jews. In Europe, the libel was that Jews used the blood of Christian children for ritual purposes. In Islam, the libel is that Jews are desecrating Al-Aqsa Mosque and planning to destroy it. This round of the libel is being propelled by Qatar, Turkey, Hamas and the Muslim Brotherhood. In both libels, the goal was/is incitement to kill Jews. After rejecting the UN partition plan in 1948, Arab nations attacked Israel in a war clearly declared as genocide. Israel survived. Egypt and Jordan had no interest in creating a Palestinian Arab state, yet the Arabs attacked again in 1967. Israel wanted peace. It magnanimously gave the Jordanian government control over the Mount where the Dome and the Mosque stood. Jerusalem is holy to Jews, Christians and Muslims. Arab perfidy and terror must be denounced.

Iran, Not North Korea, Is Biggest Risk To Peace
Belfast Telegraph, September 15, 2017

In 1994, Bill Clinton gave North Korea $5 bn and two nuclear reactors, hoping to curb its push to nuclear weaponization.

In 2015, Barak Obama led the way to legitimize and fund Iran's nuclear ambitions and dreams of world hegemony.

Today's crisis on the Korean peninsula is the preview of the real battle to come. Korea is a regional threat. Iran had grander designs.

Iran is intensely watching the jousting between Donald Trump and Kim Jong-un. If the West blinks and North Korea is allowed to have its nuclear arsenal, Iran will be unstoppable.

Iran and its proxies have carried out attacks in Argentina, the Middle East, North Africa and elsewhere. It would gladly sacrifice a few million shahids in the conflagration with Israel.

A nuclear North Korea will guarantee a Nuclear Iran. The West will have to capitulate to the caliphate or fight. Europe has already thrown in the towel. The fate of the free world rests with America.

PLO Still Hasn't Changed
Washington Times, November 27, 2017

The 1993 Oslo accords recognized the Palestinian Liberation Organization as the sole representative of the Arabs of Palestine ("US puts Palestinians on notice: DC office may be shuttered.") This terrorist group was supposed to change its spots, but it has not.

In return for ignoring other Arab leaders and factions, it was invited to set up headquarters in Ramallah and to begin a peace process with Israel. It pledged to prepare the population for life alongside Israel and to end violence and enticement to violence. It also pledged not to attack Israel in international forums.

Well, it lied from day one. It has rejected every peace offer from Israel, even those offered by the Obama administration. It is apparent the PLO/Fatah has manipulated everyone. It's time for them to leave the stage. With support of major Arab-League players and the United States, the Palestinians can find new leadership. If not, they will remain the world's major welfare recipients and others will determine their fate. Likely, their neighbors will take the decision out of their hands. They only became recognized as a people in 1964, when the KGB and Egypt formed the PLO. Perhaps that experiment is over.

THE U.S. SAID 'NO'
Haaretz, December 10, 2017

The second intifada saw 1,000 Israelis murdered and 3,000 Arab terrorists killed attacking Israeli civilians. Yasser Arafat planned the intifada before going to Camp David to meet President Bill Clinton and Prime Minister Ehud Barak. Though they got everything they claimed (to the West) they wanted, Arafat feared signing an "end of conflict clause" would lead to his death, so he went home and launched his suicide bombers.

The Israelis learned, built the security barrier and can somewhat control the flow of people from the West Bank.

The Arabs riot when their leaders tell them to, when they are angry and when they are happy. Every riot is a party.

Israel had been the capital of the Jews for over 3,000 years, when King David built his temple. Jews ruled Jerusalem several times over the millennia. It has never been an Arab capital.

In the 20th century, it always had more Jews then either Christians or Muslims, until the Jordanians illegally occupied it from 1949 to 1967 and killed or forced them out.

Trump, stating the obvious, has motivated the Arabs. They have long ago stopped pretending that every inch of Israel is not occupied Palestinian territory. Now, the United States has said "No."

The Muslim world, including the Organization of Islamic Cooperation and the Arab League, can shed the dream they will eventually "drive the Jews into the sea." It is time for them to release their brothers they have kept in squalid refugee camps for 70 years. It is time for them to make peace and join in the economic and intellectual dynamism that is Israel.

They may dominate Europe, but they will not vanquish Israel.

2018

FALSE SCENARIOS USED IN ATTEMPT TO SHAME ISRAEL
Vancouver Sun, January 4, 2018

Re: Palestinian teen indicted after soldiers slapped.

This is Pallywood. European, Israeli and Arab film crews, funded by anti-Israel NGOs, set up false scenarios, hoping to provoke incidents they can manipulate to produce propaganda videos to shame Israel. The internet then zips these lies around the world.

Palestinian parents goad their children into throwing stones at Israeli civilians and soldiers. They encourage them to harass soldiers in the hope of getting a response. The civilized world considers this to be child abuse. To terrorists and others espousing anti-Semitism, these coerced children are heroes.

'REFUGEE FUNDS' DON'T GO TO PALESTINIANS
Washington Times, January 15, 2018

The United Nations Relief and Works Agency for Palestinian Refugees in the Near East (UNRWA) has exacerbated rather than helped the problems of refugees who still languish in squalid camps after 70 years ("The faded Palestinian issue.")

In 1948, in defiance of international law, local Arab militias and the armies of Lebanon, Syria, Iraq, Egypt, Saudi Arabia and Transjordan attacked Israel. It was a war not for a tiny piece of land, nor to create another Arab state, but one clearly defined as genocide. In consequence, 700,000 Palestinian Arabs and 10,000 Palestinian Jews were displaced. In subsequent years, another 900,000 Jews were forced out of their homes in Arab lands and Iran.

The Arab refugees and their descendants claim to now number 6.5 million, with 3.8 million registered to receive aid. Shame on the Palestinian Authority, the Arab League, the United Nations and the 30,000 members of UNRWA. UNRWA takes in $1 billion from its 15 top donors, with America contributing $380 million. Other governmental and non-governmental agencies also fund the PA. What have they to show for it?

The refugee camps in Lebanon, Syria, Jordan, Gaza and the West Bank are Arab-controlled. Between the PA and Hamas' incompetence and corruption, they have little interest in the refugees, though they have funds enough to pay terrorists to kill Jews and Americans.

So long as the United States funds them, the Palestinians have no incentive to make peace with Israel or to take responsibility for running their own affairs.

WHY IS ANYBODY STILL FUNDING THIS U.N. AGENCY?
Wall Street Journal, January 21, 2018

When the fighting ended in 1948 and the war entered into a stalemate, no Arab country was willing to take in the Palestinians.

First and foremost, aid for Palestine goes into the foreign bank accounts of its corrupt leadership. Yasser Arafat is thought to have amassed a $1 billion fortune. Next, it is used to pay terrorists. The families of anyone who has died or been imprisoned because he or she murdered Jews are celebrated and given pensions in appreciation from a grateful government. Finally, huge sums are expended on preparations for the next war "to drive the Jews into the sea."

Hamas builds tunnels into Israel for its military instead of replacing the homes and hospitals from which its fighters fired rockets.

Until aid is administered and projects supervised by donor countries, this pattern will continue.

Israel Has Beaten The Boycott Movement
Belfast Telegraph, February 2, 2018

The boycott, divest and sanction (BDS) movement is racism — pure and simple.

Israel is the one Middle Eastern haven where gay people, Christians, Baha'i, Bedouin and Africans flee to escape persecution throughout the Arab world.

Israel's neighbors hang gay people, murder infidels, defile and torch churches, treat their woman as chattels, keep slaves and have confined Palestinian Arab refugees in UN welfare camps in Gaza, the West Bank, Lebanon, Syria and Jordan for generations.

Israel is an economic and scientific dynamo. It has relations and trades with most of the world. Its growth is a magnet for investment.

BDS has been a flop. The aim of BDS is the destruction of Israel.

Pallywood Propagandist
Jerusalem Post, February 18, 2018

With regard to "UN calls on Israel to free Ahed Tamimi," Tamimi is a teenager, a delinquent and a coward. She would not dare slap and punch a Palestinian cop. She would not assault an Israeli soldier without the cameras rolling.

She was coached by her parents and has become a Pallywood propagandist. In a situation where their leaders encourage vehicular and knife attacks on Jews, she would only pout and act out in front of the media.

Let's remember, too, that Israel captured Judea and Samaria after Jordan attacked it. Jordan had illegally occupied the territory since 1949, forcing out all the Jews. It did not consider the Palestinian Arabs a distinct group, so it never created a state for them.

SUFFERING GAZA
Haaretz, March 14, 2018

Re: White House to Hold Talks on Gaza Crises With Officials From Israel, Arab World, Europe.

Of course it was unlikely that the Palestinian Authority would attend these talks. The last thing Palestinian President Mahmoud Abbas and the PA want is to change the status quo in Gaza. They don't want to enhance the reputation of their rivals, Hamas. They need to keep the Gazans in misery and continue to blame it on Israel.

Billions of dollars have been poured into Gaza by the world community since Israel moved every last Jew out of the Strip in 2005. What could have been a brand-new start at developing a Palestinian entity descended into chaos, violence and corruption.

Calm could threaten Abbas' new $20 million home in Ramallah. It might endanger the cut he takes out of every contract. It might signal the end of his reign and of his family's income. Furthermore, he has no intention of living alongside Israel.

For all his huffing and puffing, Abbas is still just one of the little pigs.

JERUSALEM IMPORTANT FOR JEWS, NOT MUSLIMS
Belfast Telegraph, March 22, 2018

It is time we told Mahmoud Abbas, the Palestinian president, that we know the truth: Jerusalem is not, nor has it ever been, an important Muslim site, in spite of what the United Nations, UNESCO and other international organs postulate.

Jerusalem became King David's capital just over 3,000 years ago.

His son, Solomon, built the First Temple there. Jerusalem was, and is, the soul of Judaism. When the Jewish slaves fled Pharaoh's Egypt in 1250 BC they made their way back to their holy land.

Christianity grew out of Judaism. Jesus was a Jew and his gospels took place in and around Jerusalem. So, Christians have a two millennium-long attachment with Jerusalem.

When the Arabs spread out of Arabia (also adopting the Jewish and Christian stories) in the 7th century, Jerusalem was never their capital, Ramle was. Yes, they built the Dome of the Rock atop the ruins of the Second Temple and the al-Aqsa mosque off to the side of the Mount. The Dome is beautiful, but the site pales in comparison to the fabulous structures they built in Cairo, Casablanca, Istanbul and elsewhere.

The Babylonians, Romans, Arabs, Christians and others never considered Jerusalem important enough to make it a capital, but it was the Jewish capital whenever they had dominance over it. Today, Muslims want it only because the Jews have it.

WORLD'S PATIENCE WITH HAMAS IS RUNNING OUT
Belfast Telegraph, April 9, 2018

HAMAS is forcing people to camp out and riot along the border with Israel. Gazans should be camping by the sea instead of at the border. The beaches were a glorious playground only a few years ago. Now the shore is a polluted blight.

Israel isn't going away. Israel has one of the most advanced societies on earth. Israeli Arabs are the freest in the world and are blossoming. Hamas's goal of destroying Israel would not elevate the Arabs living there or in the disputed West Bank. As in the rest of the Middle East and North Africa, where the ordinary people live in poverty and ignorance, Gazans would fare no better.

So, whining about 'the Nakba' and the other wars the Arabs launched against Israel and lost won't move them forward.

Right now, while the world is still accustomed to supporting them, is the time to clean up their act and make peace with Israel. More and more countries are becoming fed up with Hamas's waste and corruption and are cutting back their donations.

And, by the way, the United Nations defines an Arab refugee as anyone who lived in Mandatory Palestine for two years.

Also, where is UN outrage over the 1,000,000 Jews forced out of Arab lands?

A REAL PEACE WITHOUT THE PLO
New York Daily News, May 5, 2018

Mahmoud Abbas' anti-Semitic rant has finally unmasked him. He is unfit for dealing with Israel in any capacity. It is time for him to retire to his $20 million home in Ramallah and for the Arab League to take control of the disputed territories. The Arab League was responsible for the 1948, 1967 and 1973 wars of genocide against Israel. Well, times have changed. Iran is the existential threat to both Israel and the Sunni states. It occupies Lebanon, via Hezbollah and parts of Syria with Russian backing.

Hamas, which turned Gaza from a potential economic success into a hell-hole, is also an Iranian client. Hamas is part of the Muslim Brotherhood and is supported by CAIR and the Muslim Students' Associations in our universities. All are rabidly racist and promote violence.

The United Nations, dominated by the 57 votes of the Organization of Islamic Cooperation, is useless. While most of its members recognize and deal with Israel commercially, they vote against or abstain in UN committees. This charade can go on forever, but it will not solve the Palestinian problem.

The PLO was founded in 1964 to use terrorism as a political tool to drive infidels out of the Middle East and North Africa. The PLO and its offshoots, the PA and Hamas, have failed. The leadership enriched itself, a middle-class did emerge, but for most Palestinians, particularly those in refugee camps, life on welfare has been brutal.

The EU elites are making too much money dealing with Iran to care about the Palestinians or that their own cultures will soon be submerged under the Islamic invasion.

Only the Arab League, backed by the United States, can influence the creation of two states, one Palestinian and one Jewish, living in peace side-by-side.

Palestinians Need Reality Check
Irish Independent, May 21, 2018

What is wrong with the Arabs who have called themselves "Palestinians" since 1964, when the PLO was founded in Egypt to get rid of infidels in MENA (Middle East and North Africa)?

In the British mandate for Palestine, only Jews were called Palestinians. Have today's Palestinians not figured out no one cares about them? Do they not remember that in the 1948 war, Egypt took Gaza and Jordan occupied the West Bank? Why did they not start "Palestine"? The answer is they recognized no Arabs called Palestinians. Their goal was to drive out the infidels and split up the land. Now is the best time for the Palestinians to join Israel and set up a two-state solution. Now, while non-Arabs are still willing to pay, and while Iran and Hezbollah are being kept at bay, they can make a deal with Israel. They can enjoy the prosperity their Israeli Arab brothers enjoy and develop the best society in all of MENA. With the West paying and Israel co-operating, they have the opportunity to succeed.

But this means throwing off the psychopaths who run Fatah and Hamas, accepting the Jewish state of Israel and acknowledging if Israel were to be destroyed, there would still never be a place called Palestine.

The UNHRC Scam
Haaretz, July 4, 2018

It is almost totally "people of color" who are being persecuted under the supposedly protective cover of the UN Human Rights Council.

The UNHRC, like every other United Nations body, is controlled by the 56-state bloc of the Organization of Islamic Cooperation. Nothing happens without their approval, including seats and chairmanships on councils, commissions and nonprofit organizations.

The OIC is easy to please. To it, the UN's function is to funnel money from the few wealthy Western democracies into the coffers of third-world dictators and to those entities willing to play ball with the OIC. Aside from the unearned redistribution of wealth, participating in the delegitimization and destruction of the state of Israel is essential.

The UNHRC is the perfect foil. Its membership comes largely from the most vicious human rights abusers. By focusing primarily on the only Jewish state and one which has a strong, free and open government and judiciary, they shield their own members and their friends from the scrutiny and condemnation they deserve.

Every self-respecting, free society should shun the UNHRC for the scam that it is.

CAN THE PALESTINIAN AMBASSADOR TO THE U.S. SURVIVE THE TRUMP ERA?
Moment Magazine, July 7, 2018

Yes. The PLO, founded by Egypt and the KGB in 1964 to drive the infidels out of the Middle East, can survive if they face reality.

They managed to throw 700,000 Christians out of Lebanon, but the Jews and Christians are thriving in Israel, along with approximately 1.75 million Muslims.

In 1993, behind the backs of the Israeli and American governments, Yitzhak Rabin and Yasser Arafat signed the Oslo Accords. Arafat was to convert from terrorist to diplomat and be the sole representative of the Palestinian Arabs. He was welcomed to set up a working capital in Ramallah and to engage in a peace project with Israel.

Obviously, Arafat lied. The original goal of the PLO was unchanged. He died, a wealthy man, without a country.

Now, many years later, his successor, Mahmoud Abbas, enjoying his $20,000,000 home in Ramallah, will likely also end his career, country-less.

There are two things the PLO must accept. First, they do not represent all the people they claim to represent. Hamas has a huge following. And, second, and most important, they have failed miserably.

They failed to push out the Infidels.

They failed to even start to create the foundations of an independent state.

All they did was create a kleptocracy, where the elites became super-rich and the peasants suffered.

They brought repeated wars and death upon the region, to no avail.

Now, they must stop. They must lay down their weapons. They must accept what they, other Palestinian Arabs, the Israelis and the Arab League can work out.

Trump cannot impose his will on them, any more than could Obama, who leaned heavily in their favor.

The PLO will survive if they accept Israel as a Jewish state they can co-exist with. The alternate will be more fighting, until the Israelis finally defeat them totally and impose a peace on them.

HAMAS CANNOT BE FREE TO TERRORIZE ISRAELIS
Belfast Telegraph, July 23, 2018

Israel does not want control of another people; nor does it wish to be destroyed. The goal of Hamas is the elimination of Israel. They have pledged repeatedly to not recognize Israel as a Jewish state and to insist on allowing millions of Arabs into Israel.

What the Arabs want is to get as much as they can without agreeing to a permanent peace treaty.

Hamas has been firing rockets into Israel for years. They started this round of hostilities in an attempt to develop credibility within the Islamist community. Just as al-Qaeda became prominent on 9/11, Hamas is attempting to break out of the rut it finds itself in.

Hamas is bankrupt. It lost its easy access to goods, materials and weapons smuggled in from Sinai. Even though Hamas and Fatah have signed an agreement, Fatah won't pay Gaza's public servants' salaries.

Hamas and Hezbollah were fighting each other in Syria, so another support link has been severed. Hamas' only steadfast ally is Iran.

If Hamas can score a major hit in Tel Aviv, or Jerusalem, it will become important again and funding will start pouring in from Islamic charities around the world. It is Israel's job to make sure Hamas fails.

The fawning EU and UN must not give Hamas another chance to terrorize the Israelis and Palestinian Arabs.

LOOKING ON THE BRIGHT SIDE OF THE CANADA-SAUDI SPAT
Vancouver Sun, August 10, 2018

Little Canada has finally grown a spine. We reprimanded the Saudis for human rights violations and they were not amused. Excellent. We win.

So, they won't sell us oil. Good. Now we'll start depending on North American supplies. They'll pull their students from our schools and, hopefully, their money too. Our universities have been polluted by their cash, not that our left-wing academia didn't fit right in with their radical ideology.

The downside for our prime minister is he won't get the seat on the UN Security Council that he has dreamed of. Without the backing of the 56-member Organization of Islamic Cooperation, Canada can kiss that goodbye, one less entanglement in that international swamp. Makes one proud, eh?

UNRWA SHOULD BE ABOLISHED
Haaretz, October 8, 2018

So now most UNRWA staff have fled into Israel, chased out by Hamas mobs. It reminds one of the Hamas/Palestinian Authority civil war when PA supporters and Bedouin were forced out in 2007 and sought safety in Israel.

UNRWA, the biggest "refugee" scam in history, has helped keep the Arabs under its control in poverty while supporting the terrorist agenda.

UNRWA was supposed to help the 700,000 Arabs who fled or were forced out of their homes in the 1948 war of genocide against the Jews, but not one refugee has been permanently resettled and taken off the welfare rolls in 70 years. That is a scandal.

Contrast this behavior with the situation of the 1 million Jews forces out of Arab lands and Iran. Most were welcomed into the newly created Israel and given new, productive lives. These Jewish refugees and their descendants make up 50% of Israel's population.

UNRWA should be abolished and UNHCR should assume responsibility for all the world's refugees.

Not My Idea Of Human Rights
Haaretz, September 23, 2018

Re: B'Tselem head to UN: Time has come for action.

Who defined B'Tselem as Israel's leading human rights group?

Was it self-defined or was it the European Union, which funds it and the illegal construction of Arab settlements in the disputed territories?

Hamas and the Palestinian Authority have separated the Gaza Strip from Judea and Samaria (the West Bank). Their civil war in 2007 put Hamas in power and drove PA supporters and Bedouin into Israel for safe haven.

It must be noted that the term "Palestinian" was only applied to Arabs after the PLO was established by Egypt and the former Russian secret police and intelligence agency, the KGB, in 1964. Prior to that, only Jews were called "Palestinians." Also, Gazans are mostly Egyptians, while West Bank Arabs are primarily from Jordan and Syria.

B'Tselem is a foreign-funded group with a strange concept of "human rights." Its main function is to discredit Israel.

It has also worked to entrap Arabs who sold or who planned to sell land to Jews, a capital offense under the PA. Those turned in to the PA can expect torture and execution.

That is not my idea of human rights.

And Then They Came For Me
Washington Times, October 30, 2018

Anti-Semitism flourishes on both the far right and the far left ("Pittsburgh mourns with Jewish community, says 'hatred will never win out.'") On the right are the neo-Nazis and their European-style traditional racism. They are small in number and are mostly inconsequential today.

On the left are Louis Farrakhan (not shunned by America's left, including Barack Obama and Hillary Clinton), Black Lives Matter and our universities. Universities are spurred on by left-leaning professors and the Muslim Students' Association (MSA), which sponsors BDS,

Israel Apartheid Week and other so-called pro-Palestinian activities. MSA is part of the Muslim Brotherhood, as is Hamas.

Black Lives Matter has hooked up with MSA, making it part of the anti-Semitism plaguing America.

It seems the more left/progressive a person, the more likely they are to be anti-American, anti-white and anti-Semitic, regardless of their ethnicity.

The world's oldest hatred has become socially acceptable again. History has shown that attacks against Jews soon spread to others. If left unchecked, Western democracies will be imperiled.

BOOT HAMAS FROM GAZA
Washington Times, November 20, 2018

Following the 2014 Hamas-Israel conflict, the United Nations (no friend of Israel) reported that Israel had a right to prevent weapons getting into Gaza. After the recent weeks of attacks on Israel's Gaza border and the firing of 500 rockets in one day, including tank missiles, at Israeli civilian targets, there can be no further disagreement that Israel is fully justified in its embargo.

Article 7 of the Hamas charter calls for the death of every Jew on Earth. Hamas is the Palestinian chapter of the Muslim Brotherhood, whose other branches include CAIR and the Muslim Students' Association chapters at many of our universities.

Funding by the Muslim Brotherhood, its associates, the European Union and other nations hostile to Israel, has kept Hamas in power since 2007. Only the Palestinian Authority withholds payments from them.

It's time Hamas is recognized as the genocidal war criminals they are. For the sake of the people of Gaza, Hamas must be removed.

ANTI-SEMITISM IS EASY TO RECOGNIZE
Belfast Telegraph, November 30, 2018

IF there is a double-standard when discussing Israel (or Jews) and other countries (or people), if Israel is being demonized, or if calls are made for Israel's destruction, then that is anti-Semitism.

The International Holocaust Remembrance Alliance has provided a guide for recognizing anti-Semitism.

Contemporary examples of anti-Semitism in public life, the media, schools, the workplace and in the religious sphere could, taking into account the overall context, include — but are not limited to:

Calling for, aiding, or justifying the killing, or harming, of Jews in the name of a radical ideology, or an extremist view of religion;

Making mendacious, dehumanizing, demonizing, or stereotypical allegations about Jews, or the power of Jews as a collective — such as the myth about a world Jewish conspiracy, or of Jews controlling the media;

Accusing Jews as a people of being responsible for real, or imagined, wrongdoing committed by a single Jewish person, or group, or even for acts committed by non-Jews;

Denying the fact, scope, mechanisms (for example, gas chambers) or intentionality of the genocide of the Jewish people at the hands of National Socialist Germany and its supporters and accomplices during the Second World War (the Holocaust);

Accusing the Jews as a people, or Israel as a state, of inventing, or exaggerating, the Holocaust.

LET EUROPE SERVE AS LESSON
Washington Times, December 17, 2018

Europe is being destroyed by uncontrolled migration. There are refugees, fake refugees, economic migrants and terrorists, and no one can identify who is who.

Most are not looking to integrate into their host countries. They are colonists. Their aim is to overwhelm Western societies. Hundreds of sharia courts function in every major European city and there are numerous no-go zone, where infidels are forced out and police will not enter.

Jews are not safe in Europe and are leaving in record numbers, particularly from France, England, Norway and Sweden, where authorities cannot or will not protect them.

We must all be compassionate and ease the suffering of genuine refugees, but America would be foolish to follow Europe's example.

"Whoever would change men must change the conditions of their lives." —Theodor Herzl

2019

SAY BYE-BYE TO BDS
Washington Times, January 11, 2019

Leave it to Sen. Chuck Schumer to try and improve his street creds with progressives by threatening Israel ("Senate Democrats back BDS anti-Israel movement with filibuster of Mideast partnership bill," Web, Jan. 8). American-Israeli interests should not be made into a partisan issue. Mr. Schumer is sending the wrong message to the new Congress.

The Boycott, Divestment and Sanctions (BDS) movement promotes itself as a grassroots movement. It is anything but. It is a well-funded, anti-Semitic organization dedicated to the destruction of the Jewish state. The cries of BDS supporters have nothing to do with downtrodden Palestinians. If they have cared about the Arab refugees since 1948, why have they allowed them to fester in fetid refugee camps in Gaza, the West Bank, Lebanon, Jordan and Syria for all these years?

Israeli Arabs are the only free Arabs in the Middle East and North Africa. The Arab List is the third largest group in the Knesset and an Arab sits on Israel's Supreme Court. Israeli hospitals and universities serve everyone. Arab women are equal under the law to their male family members. In Israel, gays are not thrown off buildings, as they are in Gaza.

Large numbers of Arabs migrated to Palestine in the 1920s and '30s at the urging of Haj Amin al Husseini, Hitler's ally, to thwart the Zionist enterprise and for work. To call an Arab a Palestinian was an insult. Only Jews were Palestinians.

It was in 1964, when the KGB and Egypt founded the PLO, that the myth of "historic Palestine" was created.

The original Arab mistake was to not welcome the hard-working Jews, who drained the malarial swamps and made the deserts bloom.

What progress could have been brought to a region still wallowing in poverty and tribal hostilities?

BDS is one aspect of Islamic supremacist ideology. It is part of the rapid spread of Islam across the West. It is being pumped into the supple minds of our young university students.

BDS should be shunned.

THERE ARE NO 'OCCUPIED LANDS'
Irish Examiner, January 30, 2019

To begin with, there are no "occupied lands" in the former British Mandate for Palestine. According to the Oslo Accords (signed by the government of Israel and the Palestinian Liberation Organization in 1993, and again in 1995), the land under discussion is "disputed territory" until such time as the Arab-Israeli conflict is settled and borders are finalized.

In the territories, there are many businesses and industrial parks, owned by both Muslims and Jews, and employing thousands of Muslims and Jews working together. Boycotting these businesses will throw employees out of work. Arabs in these companies earn pay equal to those in Israel, which are many times higher than they could earn in the Arab sector.

Would Ireland boycott Turkey-occupied Cyprus or Chinese-occupied Tibet?

If not, you have to challenge your prejudices.

The world-wide Boycott, Divestment, Sanctions Movement clearly states its goal is the destruction of Israel. And, finally, as you wonder how Ireland will be treated, remember, one good boycott deserves another: Will I ever visit Ireland again?

SACRED TO ISLAM? NO.
Jerusalem Post, February 1, 2019

Arab leaders know the truth. Jerusalem is not, nor has it ever been, an important Muslim site ("Is Jerusalem a sacred Islamic city?").

Abraham, the first Jew, purchased his burial place in Hebron around 4,000 years ago. Jewish slaves, fleeing Pharaoh in 1250 BC, made their way back home.

Jerusalem became King David's capital just over 3,000 years ago and his son Solomon built the First Temple there. Jerusalem was and is the soul of Judaism.

When the Arabs spread out of Arabia in the 7th century, they conquered the Middle East, North Africa, much of the Far East and parts of Europe. Jerusalem was never one of their capitals. Nearby Ramle was.

Babylonians, Romans, Arabs, Christians and others did not consider Jerusalem important enough to make it a capital, but the Jews did whenever they had dominance over it

Today the Sunni Arabs rely on Israel to keep Turkey from re-establishing its Ottoman Empire and Iran from taking over, but in public they bluster and condemn Israel in unison.

No Room for Bigotry: Omar's Inexcusable Tweets
New York Post, February 13, 2019

No, Nancy: An unequivocal apology is not good enough. That Omar and Tlaib are bigots is a stain on the Democratic Party. They should have been vetted and ejected from the party long before the elections.

Omar cannot apologize away her anti-Semitism. Speaker Pelosi must do the right thing or acknowledge that her party is OK with a bigoted component. The very least the speaker can do is ensure these two congresswomen are not members of any committee.

In the next election, Minnesota and Michigan voters can select more appropriate representation.

Don't Punish Israel
Sun Sentinel Palm Beach, February 24, 2019

Authors Alan Levine and Donna Nevel are wrong on punishing Airbnb over Israeli decision.

They set up a false scenario and then proceed to attack Israel and its supporters.

To correct their errors, there are no such thing as "illegal Israeli settlements built on occupied Palestinian land in the West Bank."

There are Israeli bedroom communities and several industrial parks that supply high-paying jobs to Jews and Arabs in the disputed territories.

Where were these so-called settlements during the 1948 and 1967 wars of genocide against the Jews? There were none, so they are not the "core of the dispute."

The core issue is the Arab refusal to allow any infidel entity to be self-governing in any place once under Islamic control. This includes the former Islamic colonies of Spain, Portugal and other parts of Europe.

Airbnb has joined the BDS movement, whose stated goal is the destruction of Israel and the euthanizing (their word) of Jews everywhere. BDS is part of the Muslim Brotherhood whose plan is the replacement of the Christian world with a caliphate. Its Middle East wing is Hamas.

Levine and Nevel are misguided, or worse.

Get rid of Omar now
The Washington Times, March 5, 2019

Surely it is time Minnesota Democratic Congresswoman Ilhan Omar was thrown out of the Democratic Party ("Ilhan Omar repeats anti-Semitic trope against Jewish congresswoman," Web, March 3). At a minimum, she should be relieved of her position on the House Foreign Affairs Committee.

She is a disgrace to Congress and to the Muslim Americans she claims to represent. I am sure her constituents are not all anti-Semites.

Ms. Omar's racism is so ingrained in her core that she is unaware of the vile statements she repeatedly makes.

House Speaker Nancy Pelosi must take action or own the charge her party tolerates racism.

Pelosi will pay for inaction
Boston Herald, March 10, 2019

Nancy Pelosi's failure to act quickly and decisively to shut down the racism in her party bodes ill for democracy and she will pay for it in 2020. Her freshmen stars, Ocasio-Cortez, Omar and Tlaib and the Congressional Black Caucus are a disgrace. A resolution condemning anti-Semitism should have been overwhelmingly approved with minimal pushback, but it was not.

The American-Israeli relationship has never been a partisan issue. It is based on mutual values and respect. American Jews are loyal Democrats by a 3 to 1 margin. Will some now rethink their position?

Ocasio-Cortez is simply ignorant. Is she really comparing anti-Semitism with statements that are homophobic, anti-Latinx or anti-blackness?

In my lifetime, one out of every three Jews in the world were murdered by anti-Semites. No other group, except for gays living in Islamic countries, has faced this level of danger.

If only more countries were as brave as Israel
Belfast Telegraph, April 4, 2019

The EU is enraged. Tiny Israel has the fortitude to stand up to the Islamic juggernaut, while Europeans are watching their countries and cultures being swamped.

As for UN resolutions against the seizure of land by force, they have it backwards.

International law states a nation cannot keep land seized in an aggressive action. However, Syria was the aggressor. Israel defended itself in a war of genocide launched against it. Self-defense is not a hostile act. It is the core reason for the existence of nations.

Israel is America's aircraft carrier. It provides the US with billions of dollars in technical upgrades to its military equipment.

It is America's eyes and ears in a violent sea of dictatorships. It shares America's values.

'Eurabia' will try to protect its fragile business contracts for as long as possible, but its fate is precarious.

BETO VS. BIBI
New York Post, April 14, 2019

What less would we expect of Robert Francis O'Rourke ("Prez hopeful Beto blasts 'racist' Netanyahu," April 8)?

O'Rourke is one in a crowd of Democrats trying to be more radical than the extreme leftwing new congresswomen in order to stand out.

He is a typical progressive: anti-American, anti-white and anti-Semitic. So, as a self-loathing white man who wants to eliminate all physical borders, he labels Israeli Prime Minister Benjamin Netanyahu a racist.

THE WINNER IS...US
Jerusalem Post, April 15, 2019

As I read "Palestinian officials: Israelis voted to maintain apartheid" (April 11) I realized Saeb Erekat would be just as distressed by whoever won Israel's election. He is distressed that Israel is the only liberal democracy in the Middle East and North Africa (MENA.)

Where in MENA are Arabs better off than in Israel? Netanyahu did not say he would annex territory. He said he would extend Israeli law to certain Israeli towns in the West Bank.

Even Hanan Ashrawi must acknowledge there never was a "Palestine" until the British Mandate, after WWI and until 1948, only Jews were called Palestinians. The local Arabs called themselves Egyptians or Syrians or just Arabs. In 1948, 50% of Palestinian Arabs were newcomers who migrated to the region in search of the employment opportunities created by the Jews and at the urging of Grand Mufti al-Husseini.

Shortly after 1948, 50% of Israelis were Jewish refugees expelled from Arab lands.

20% of Israel is Arab. 19% of Israeli medical students are Arab. 20% of Israeli doctors and pharmacists and 25% of its nurses are Arab. The Arab List is the 3rd largest group in the Knesset. An Arab sits on Israel's Supreme Court.

That is not apartheid. That is citizenship.

Afterword

The story of Arabs and their relations with Jews started in the 7th century with the birth of Muhammad and the creation of Islam.

It is one of conquest by the Arabs and submission of the Jews under their control.

A similar fate befell Christians and other infidels Islam had dominance over throughout the centuries.

Since the mid-1800's, when Jews outnumbered both Christians and Muslims in Jerusalem, Zionism, the desire and necessity for Jews to become self-sufficient in their ancient homeland, began to percolate.

In the 20th century, two cataclysms, the Muslim Brotherhood and Nazism, emerged to challenge the world, and particularly the Jews.

These letters are my record of the Arab-Israeli conflict and its effect on the world during the 20th and the beginning of the 21st centuries.

They were written with hope.

Lightning Source UK Ltd.
Milton Keynes UK
UKHW041604080519
342323UK00001B/497/P